2

Detroit Studies in Music Bibliography

SIR ARTHUR S. SULLIVAN

WILLIAM S. GILBERT

Sir Arthur Sullivan:
AN INDEX TO THE TEXTS
OF HIS VOCAL WORKS

Compiled by
Sirvart Poladian
Music Division
The New York Public Library

1961

Detroit Studies in Music Bibliography

Number 2

Published by
INFORMATION SERVICE, INCORPORATED
10 West Warren   Detroit 1, Michigan

PHOTOLITHOPRINTED BY CUSHING - MALLOY, INC.
ANN ARBOR, MICHIGAN, UNITED STATES OF AMERICA
1961

TABLE OF CONTENTS

PREFACE

An attempt has been made to list every title and first line, repeated catchy refrains, and important musical sections in the operettas and
other larger vocal works of Sir Arthur Sullivan.

A separate section is devoted to the single songs, hymns and
anthems composed or arranged by Sullivan.

Inasmuch as the published versions of the operettas exhibit
considerable minor variations, interpolations and omissions customary in
this genre, the compiler makes no claim that this index is absolutely complete or perfect; but it is perhaps by far the most comprehensive list published so far, containing approximately 3,000 entries.

The extensive collection of Sullivan's music at the Music
Division of the New York Public Library served as the primary source in
the preparation of this Index. I am grateful to this Library, as are thou-
sands of others each year, for making the wealth of its resources available.

For his assistance and for making the files of his Sullivan
collection at the Pierpont Morgan Library available for consultation, I am
grateful to Mr. Reginald Allen. For advice and assistance I am also in-
debted to Mr. William Lichtenwanger of The Library of Congress and Mr.
Herbert Cahoon of the Morgan Library.

In addition to these libraries the following lists and indices
proved useful:
Grove's Dictionary of Music and Musicians.... 5th ed.
   New York, St. Martin's Press, 1955. vol. 8
Hughes, Gervase.
   The music of Arthur Sullivan. London, Macmillan, 1960.
Pazdirek, Franz.
   Universal-Handbuch der Musik-literatur aller Zeiten und
   Völker... Vienna [1904-1910] v. 29.
Sullivan, Herbert and Newman Flower.
   Sir Arthur Sullivan... 2nd. ed. London, Cassel & Co.
   [1950] (List of Works compiled by William C. Smith)

BIOGRAPHICAL SKETCH

Arthur Seymour Sullivan was born in London on May 13, 1842, to a Professor at the Royal Military Academy of Music and his wife Maria Clementina, who also came from a musical family.

At an early age Arthur Sullivan entered the Chapel Royal as chorister, where he acquired an excellent musical foundation. In 1856 he became the first recipient of the Mendelssohn Scholarship, which enabled him to study at the Royal Academy of Music with Sterndale Bennett, John Goss and others. The same scholarship permitted Sullivan to attend the Leipzig Conservatory (1858-1861) where he received comprehensive training in composition, conducting, and piano.

The incidental music to Shakespeare's Tempest he composed while in Leipzig was performed at the Crystal Palace in 1862, initiating his life-long renown. Sullivan served as organist in several of the well-known churches in London, taught at the Royal Academy of Music, conducted, and composed.

In 1867 Sir George Grove and Sullivan set out for Vienna in quest of undiscovered Franz Schubert manuscripts, and to their supreme satisfaction they found (among other items) parts of the Rosamunde music, the Symphony in C Major, and the Symphony in C Minor, the Tragic.

Then followed the collaboration with William Schwenck Gilbert, whose delectable ridicule of contemporary social manners and mores became the rage in England and the United States. The Gilbert and Sullivan craze became so intensive in America that in 1879 they crossed the Atlantic in order to combat pirated performances and editions of their operettas. It is related that H. M. S. Pinafore
"was presented at every theatre and every Concert Company of importance in the big Cities, producing the same piece without the author and composer receiving a farthing for their work. "
The first public performance of The Pirates of Penzance was given at the Fifth Avenue Theatre in New York on December 30, 1879.

Sullivan set to music texts of more serious nature, and texts by authors other than Gilbert. The opera Ivanhoe, to a libretto by Julian Sturgis, and the cantata The Golden Legend of Tennyson, contain music

VIII

well worth revival.

Although gifted in writing for the orchestra, only a limited number of compositions for instruments (between twenty and twenty-five) came from Sullivan's pen, the two major works being the Symphony in E and the violoncello concerto.

Sullivan was knighted in 1883 and honored in death (d. November 22, 1900) when he was laid to rest at St. Paul's Cathedral, London.

Amor am Bord see H.M.S. Pinafore

Beauty Stone, The   A. W. Pinero and Comyns Carr
Bunthorne's Bride see Patience

Castle Adamant see Princess Ida
Caves of Carrig-Cleena, The see
    Emerald Isle
Chieftain, The (enlarged version   F. C. Burnand
    of Contrabandista)
Contrabandista, The or The Lord of
    the Landrones see The Chieftain   F. C. Burnand
Cox and Box   F. C. Burnand, from Maddison
                                          Morton's "Box and Cox"

Emerald Isle, The or The Caves of   Basil Hood
    Carrig-Cleena (unfin., completed
    by Edward German)
Exhibition Ode   Alfred, Lord Tennyson

Flowers of Progress, The see Utopia
Foresters, The or Robin Hood and his   Alfred, Lord Tennyson
    Maid Marian (incidental music)

Gods Grown old, The see Thespis
Golden Legend, The (cantata)   Henry W. Longfellow, arr. by
                                          Joseph Bennett
Gondoliers, The or The King of   W. S. Gilbert
    Barataria
Grand Duke, The or The Statutory   W. S. Gilbert
    Duel

H. M. S. Pinafore or The Lass that   W. S. Gilbert
    Loved a Sailor (Amor am Bord)
Haddon Hall   Sidney Grundy
Henry VIII (incidental music)   Shakespeare

L'Ile enchantee (ballet)   (music lost?)
Imperial Institute Ode   Lewis Morris

London, Savoy Theatre	May 28, 1898
London, Savoy Theatre	December 12, 1894
London, St. George's Hall	December 18, 1867
London, Moray Lodge	April 27, 1867
London, Savoy Theatre	April 27, 1901
London, Albert Hall	May 4, 1886
New York, Daly's Theatre	March 25, 1892
Leeds Festival	October 16, 1885
London, Savoy Theatre	December 7, 1889
London, Savoy Theatre	March 7, 1896
London, Opera Comique	May 25, 1878
London, Savoy Theatre	September 24, 1892
Manchester, Prince's Theatre	August 29, 1877
London, Covent Garden	May 16 (14?), 1864
London, Imperial Institute	July 4, 1887

XII

London, Savoy Theatre	November 25, 1882
London, Royal English Opera House (now Palace Theatre)	January 31, 1891
Birmingham Festival	September 8, 1864
London, Lyceum Theatre	January 12, 1895
Birmingham Festival	August 27, 1873
London, Lyceum Theatre	December 29, 1888
Leeds Festival	October 15, 1880
Manchester, Prince's Theatre	September 19, 1871
London, Gaiety Theatre	December 19, 1874
London, Savoy Theatre	March 14, 1885
London, Albert Hall	May 1, 1871
London, Opera Comique	April 23, 1881
Paignton, Bijou Theatre (copyright perf.)	December 30, 1879
New York, Fifth Avenue Theatre	December 31, 1879
London, Amphitheatre	April 3, 1880
London, Savoy Theatre	January 5, 1884
Worcester Festival	September 8, 1869

* MOUNTEBANKS, comic opera, listed by Pazdirek is probably an error.
Alfred Cellier (1844-1891) composed the music for W.S. Gilbert's libretto
of that title.

London, Savoy Theatre   November 29, 1899

London, Savoy Theatre   January 22, 1887

Not produced; only the Overture   July 11, 1866
    played at St. James's Hall

London, Opera Comique   November 17, 1877

London, Chrystal Palace   April 5, 1862
London, Gaiety Theatre   December 26, 1871

London, Royalty Theatre   March 25, 1875

London, Savoy Theatre   October 7, 1893

London, Alhambra Theatre for   May 25, 1897
    Queen Victoria's Diamond Jubilee

London, Savoy Theatre   October 3, 1888

London, St. James's Theatre   June 5, 1875

Key to Abbreviations

Beauty Stone, The	Beauty
Chieftain, The	Chieftain
Contrabandista	Contrab
Cox and Box	Cox
Emerald Isle, The	Emerald
Foresters, The	Foresters
Golden Legend, The	Legend
Gondoliers, The	Gondoliers
Grand Duke, The	Grand Duke
H. M. S. Pinafore	Pinafore
Haddon Hall	Haddon
Henry VIII	Henry
Iolanthe	Iolanthe
Ivanhoe	Ivanhoe
Kenilworth	Kenilworth
King Arthur	Arthur
Light of the World, The	Light
Martyr of Antioch, The	Antioch
Merchant of Venice, The	Venice
Merry Wives of Windsor, The	Windsor
Mikado, The	Mikado
Miller and his man, The	Miller
On Shore and Sea	On Shore
Patience	Patience
Pirates of Penzance, The	Pirates
Princess Ida	Princess
Prodigal Son, The	Prodigal
Rose of Persia, The	Rose
Ruddigore	Ruddigore
Sapphire Necklace, The	Sapphire
Sorcerer, The	Sorcerer
Tempest, The	Tempest
Thespis	Thespis
Trial by Jury	Trial
Utopia Limited	Utopia
Yeomen of the Guard, The	Yeomen

XVI

The entries in Index I consist of titles and/or first lines, choruses, oft-repeated phrases and catchy musical settings within the songs in Sullivan's operettas, cantatas, and larger choral works. Considerations of economy prompted the curtailment of long first lines to dimensions sufficient for purposes of identification.

1. The Index is in strict word by word alphabetical order, except for the initial articles.

2. In accordance with usual bibliographical practice initial articles A and The have been disregarded in the alphabetical order.

3. Forms of "O" and "Oh", even though interchangeable, are listed separately as they appeared in the particular work or edition indexed. In looking for an entry consult both forms, if necessary.

4. Instances occur when these exclamations ("O", "Ah", etc.) might be added or omitted. Consult the first word following the exclamation. For example: Ah, why dost sigh and moan?
Why dost thou sigh and moan?

5. Similarly, a composer might add an extra syllable or two for musical reasons, as an anacrusis, delete others, or even change a word. Therefore minor differences arise between the original text of the libretto and the musical setting, or even between various editions of the same work. For instance: Then give three cheers
Now give three cheers

6. A prominent characteristic of Gilbert and Sullivan operettas is the rapid repartee between the soloist and chorus, during which phrases are repeated with the change of a single pronoun.
For instance: For I am an Englishman
For he is an Englishman
A few such alternatives are included in the index as sampling. The reader should bear this peculiarity in mind when trying to find an item.

7. The time required to note all variants in numerous editions and versions of Sullivan's music would be neither practical, nor justifiable. Occasionally a variant word is entered as an example of types of deviation, such as: And I have (And have I); Then (Here).

8. All acts in which an entry appears are indicated by Roman numerals; in works not divided into acts, either the Scene or the Part is cited in Arabic numbers. Princess Ida Prologue and two acts have been recorded as Act I, II, III.

GUIDE TO INDEX II

Index II contains single songs, hymns, anthems and miscellanea. Titles, first lines, hymn tune names appear in one continuous alphabetical order.

With few exceptions the main entry, giving the most complete information for any one item, is to be found under the first line of the song.

In the absence of the actual music, distinctions between title and first line could not be supplied in all instances.

Other relevant information is given within parenthesis.

Whenever easily accessible, the author of the text is mentioned.

Hymn tune names associated with Sullivan, whether original compositions or arrangements, are listed. No attempt has been made to verify the authenticity of authorship. Today hymn tune names present a state of utter confusion: the same name is applied to entirely different melodies; a given tune appears with a number of altogether unrelated texts, and other inconsistencies exist. No attempt was made to disentangle the existing complications about tune names associated with hymns published by Sullivan.

A few songs from the operettas, popularly known in sheet music form, have also been included in Index II.

Several items in the Index appear only in Pazdirek.

A few adaptations of Sullivan's tunes to new texts are included.

Tune names are underlined.
Titles are printed in capital letters.
First lines appear in regular type.

Abbreviations stand for: H - hymn
                          PS - part-song, anthem, chorus
                          T - tune name
                          W - words
                          tr. - translation

I INDEX OF FIRST LINES AND TITLES OF ALL SONGS IN THE MAJOR CHORAL WORKS

About a century since	Grand Duke I
Acclaim him who, when his true heart	Ruddigore I
Admiral's song	Pinafore I
"A British tar"	
Advertising quack, The	Mikado II
Aesthete, The	Patience I
"If you're anxious for to shine"	
After banquet, play and riot	Kenilworth
After luncheon (making merry)	Gondoliers II
After much debate internal	Patience II
After sailing to this island	Gondoliers II
After some debate internal	Patience II
Again my cursed comeliness	Patience I
Ah! as thou dost hope for mercy	Ivanhoe II
Ah! gallant soldier, brave and true	Utopia I
Ah, Holy Mother	Beauty I
Ah! in St. Patrick was a broth (by German)	Emerald II
Ah, Lady Sophy	Utopia II
Ah, leave me not to pine alone	Pirates II
Ah me! not thus did Judah's warriors go	Ivanhoe III
Ah me! what profit we	Yeomen I
Ah, must I leave thee here	Pirates II
Ah, oui, j'etais une pensionnaire	Chieftain II
Ah, pity me, my comrades true	Grand Duke I
Ah, pray make no mistake	Mikado II
Ah, the doing and undoing	Pirates II
Ah! then if he beyond the ocean foam	Ivanhoe I
Ah, well-beloved, mine angry grown	Gondoliers I
Ah! what in ambush lurks below	Legend 1
Ah, why dost sigh and moan?	Beauty III
Ah, without that thou and I	Ivanhoe III
Ah, woe is me	Legend 2
Ah woe! the poor men	Ivanhoe III
Ah, would that thou and I	Ivanhoe III
Aiaiah! Willaloo!	Iolanthe II
Air I breathe to him, The	Yeomen I
Air is charged, The	Sorcerer I
Alas! I waver to and fro!	Yeomen I
Alas! that lovers thus should meet	Sorcerer II

2

And I expect you'll all agree	Mikado I
And I have (have I) journeyed for a month	Mikado I
And I must lie like palsied monk	Ivanhoe III
And I who was once his valley-desham	Ruddigore II
And if I loved him through and through	Ruddigore I
And if you call for a song of the sea	Mikado I
And lastly I present	Utopia I
And let me stop you	Contrab II
And many a burglar I've restored	Trial
And noble Lords will scrape and bow	Gondoliers I
And now if you please, I'm ready	Trial
And now, Sergeant Bouncer	Cox
And now, Sir Conqueror	Ivanhoe I
And now, to choose our brides!	Gondoliers I
And should there come to me	Grand Duke I
And so it befell	Beauty III
And so to sleep	Ivanhoe I
And so we straight let out on bail	Mikado I
And society has always been	Rose II
And that nisi prius nuisance	Mikado I
And that's what we mean	Mikado II
And the brass will crash	Mikado I
And the world of men and women	Rose II
And the younger son	Prodigal
And then each ghost	Ruddigore II
And these we'll strike for England	Foresters II
And thus to empyrean heights	Princess II
And thus, with sinning cloyed	Ruddigore I
And we are right, I think you'll say	Mikado I
And what if it be true	Beauty I
And when amid the plaintiff's shrieks	Trial
And when he dips his royal lips	Rose II
And when he had spent all	Prodigal
And while the House of Peers withholds	Iolanthe II
And whistle all the airs.	Pirates I
And yet he witness	Ivanhoe III
And you'll allow, as I expect	Mikado I
Angelo! murderer!	Legend 4
Another wife might spoil his life	Rose I
Anyhow the man is dead	Yeomen II

3

4

Away we go to a balmy isle	Gondoliers I
Aye, Aye, my boy!	Pinafore I

Baby farming song	Pinafore II
"A many years ago"	
Bach, Spohr, Beethoven	Mikado II
Baffled grumbler, The	Princess III
"Whene'er I poke sarcastic joke"	
Banish your timidity	Yeomen I
Barcarole (Serenade)	Venice
"Mille desir"	
Baronet of Ruddigore	Ruddigore II
Barring tautology	Sorcerer I
Bat could see, A	Grand Duke I
Battle's roar is over, O my love, The	Ruddigore I
Be eloquent in praise	Patience I
Be reassured, nor fear his anger	Princess II
Bearded by these puny mortals	Iolanthe I
Beautiful English girl, The	Utopia I
"English girls of well-bred notions"	
Because I love you (by German)	Emerald II
Bedad, it's for him that we'll always employ	Emerald II
(by German)	
Bee buzzed up in the heat, The	Foresters IV
Behold, now He loved him	Light 1
Behold the lord high executioner	Mikado I
Bell trio	Pinafore II
"Never mind the why and wherefore"	
Bells are ringing o'er Mirlemont, The	Beauty I
Better than the method old	Grand Duke I
Big bombs, small bombs	Grand Duke I
Billiard sharp, The	Mikado II
Bird that breakfasts, The	Yeomen I
Blaspheme no more	Ivanhoe II
Blessed are they that are persecuted	Light 1
Blessed art Thou among women	Light 1
Blessed be the kingdom	Light 1
Blest the prince whose people's choice	On Shore

5

6

But if patriotic sentiment	Mikado I
But 'twould be an error	Princess III
But joy incessant palls the sense	Trial
But midst our jubilation	Haddon I
But owing I'm much disposed to fear	Gondoliers I
But see! what angry redness	Ivanhoe III
But still, in matters vegetable	Pirates I
But, tell me--who's the youth	Pinafore I
But the darkness has pass'd	Iolanthe II
But the liquidators say	Utopia I
But the sultan gravely thank'd him	Rose II
But they give up the felicity	Pirates I
But this he is willing to say	Trial
But though the compliment implied	Iolanthe I
But when completely rated	Ruddigore I
But when I sought her hand	Zoo
But who is this, whose god-like grace	Patience I
But youth of course must have its fling	Mikado I
Buttercup dwells on the lowly mead, The	Cox
By a simple coincidence	Patience I
By all the deer that spring	Foresters III
By all the leaves of spring	Foresters III
By Bach interwoven with Spohr	Mikado II
By heav'n, rather would I see	Ivanhoe II
By the advice of his (my) solicitor	Patience I
By the mystic regulation	Grand Duke I
By this gold chain	Ivanhoe I
By this ingenious law	Grand Duke I

Can I survive	Pinafore I
Can't find the bird	Miller 2
Capital, both--you've caught it nicely!	Gondoliers II
Care is all fiddle-de-dee	Miller Finale
Carefully on tiptoe stealing	Pinafore II
Cedric, O father, hear me pray	Ivanhoe III
Certain man had two sons, A	Prodigal
Champion, A	Ivanhoe III
Chancellor in his peruke, The	Gondoliers I

Fal-la--fal-la!	Mikado II
Fal lal la!	Iolanthe II
	Ruddigore I
Family fool, The	Yeomen II
"Oh! a private buffoon"	
Far away from toil and care	Pirates I
Far from his fetters grim	Yeomen II
Fare thee well, attractive stranger	Iolanthe I
Farewell, dear Prince, farewell	Legend 4
Farewell, my own	Pinafore II
Farewell, our gracious hostess	Haddon II
Farewell! thou hadst my heart	Ruddigore I
Fate in this has put his fingering	Gondoliers I
Fate is prickly!	Rose I
Fate of war, The	Ivanhoe II
Father, hear me	Haddon I
Father, I have sinned	Prodigal
Fear not, for behold	Light 1
Fear not, ye seek Jesus	Light 2
Fearful deed is done, The	Sorcerer II
Fickle breeze, The	Pirates II
"Sighing softly to the river"	
Fierce hussar, The	Chieftain I
Fighting is our trade	Princess I
Fill the cup	Ivanhoe I
First lord's song, The	Pinafore I
"When I was a lad"	
First, we polish off	Gondoliers II
First you're born and I'll be bound you	Utopia I
Five years have flown	Utopia I
Fix the tiger with your eye	Utopia II
Floweret shines, The	Cox
Flowers that bloom in the spring, The	Mikado II
Fold your flapping wings	Iolanthe II
For a bride's a bride	Princess II
For a fight's a kind of thing	Princess III
For a month to dwell	Princess I
For duty, duty must be done	Ruddigore I
For English girls are good as gold	Utopia I
For every time the board you spin	Grand Duke II
For ev'ry one who feels inclined	Gondoliers I

For happy the lily	Ruddigore II
For he can prophesy	Sorcerer I
For he himself has said	Pinafore II
For he's a peppr'y kind of king	Princess II
For he is an Englishman	Pinafore II
For he's going to marry Yum-Yum	Mikado I
For he's gone and married Yum-Yum	Mikado II
For he loves Little Buttercup	Pinafore II
For I'm called Little Buttercup	Pinafore I
For I am a pirate king	Pirates I
For I hold that on the seas	Pinafore I
For idleness is chief mistress (words by Henry VIII)	Henry 2, 4
For instance, this measure	Grand Duke I
For it's Terence	Emerald I
For love alone	Sorcerer I
"Love feeds on many kinds of food"	
For my military knowledge	Pirates I
For nobody can know, to a million or so	Utopia I
For now I'm a judge	Trial
For O, you vulgar vagabond	Grand Duke II
For riches and rank	Iolanthe I
For she (you are) is such a smart little craft	Ruddigore II
For the innocent joys	Emerald I
For the Lady of the Lake	Kenilworth
For the maiden fair	Princess II
For the merriest fellows are we	Gondoliers I
For thirty-five years I've been sober and wary [?]	Ruddigore II
For this musn't be, and this won't do	Utopia II
For this, my son, was dead	Prodigal
For this will be a jolly court	Grand Duke I
For Thou didst die for me	Antioch 2
For though the cup be earthen bowl	Rose I
For today our pirate 'prentice	Pirates I
For today young Alexis	Sorcerer I
For true love's sake	Haddon I
For we three, I and he	Emerald I
For years I've writh'd	Princess II
For you dream you are crossing	Iolanthe II
Forbear my friends	Yeomen I

Forbear, nor carry out	Pinafore I
Forgive, fair maid	Ivanhoe I
Free from his fetters grim	Yeomen II
Free, yet in fetters held	Yeomen II
Fremuere principes	Ivanhoe III
Friar's song, The	Ivanhoe II
"The wind blows cold"	
"Ho, jolly Jenkin"	
From bias free of every kind	Trial
From dungeon cell	Princess I
From every kind of man	Mikado II
From love a heartless jade	Yeomen I
From Mahmoud, ruler of the nation	Rose I
From morn till (to) afternoon	Yeomen I
From morning pray'r the Sultan of Persia comes	Rose II
From rock to rock	Chieftain I and Contrab I
From springtime on to summer	On Shore
From the briny sea	Ruddigore I
From the distant panorama	Princess I
From the point of view of wit	Haddon III
From the sunny Spanish shore	Gondoliers I
From the dark exile thou art summoned	Iolanthe I
Full fathom five thy father lies	Tempest I
Full many heathen in that well	Ivanhoe II
Funeral march	Arthur
"Sleep! oh, sleep! 'til night outworn"	

Gaily tripping, lightly skipping	Pinafore I
Gallant knights of old, The	Ivanhoe *
Gallant young squirrel, A	Haddon I
Gambling duet, The	Cox
"Sixes"	
Gay and gallant gondolieri	Gondoliers I
Gay hussar, The	Chieftain I
"Let us lead a life of pleasure"	
Gentle sir, my heart is frolicsome	Patience I

* Words by Chas. F. Pidgin, Music by Fred. A. Jewell. - Sheet music
published as from Sullivan's Ivanhoe.

Gently, gently, evidently	Princess II
Ghastly, ghastly! when man, sorrowful	Yeomen II
Ghosts' high noon, The	Ruddigore II
"When the night wind howls"	
Girl graduates	Princess II
"They intend to send a wire"	
Give me--now smile	Miller 2
Give thanks, give thanks to wayward Duke	Grand Duke I
(fate)	
Give us an experiment	Yeomen I
Glory, glory, glory! The Lord Almighty	
reigneth	Antioch Finale
Glory then will crown the day	Utopia II
Glory to God in the highest!	Light 1
Glory to those who battle	Ivanhoe I
Go and do your best endeavour	Pirates II
Go away, madam	Iolanthe I
Go away, young bachelor	Utopia I
Go bend the knee	Ruddigore I
Go, breaking heart	Patience I
Go, bring forth old Simon's daughter	Beauty I
Go search the world	Utopia II
Go to glory and the grave!	Pirates II
Go ye heroes, go to glory	Pirates II
Go you, and inform the lady	Princess I
God knows I pardon thee	Ivanhoe III
God sent His messenger	Legend
	Epilogue
God shall wipe away all tears	Light 2
Golden visions wave	Legend 1
Gone, and the light of my life gone with her	Legend 4
Good fellow, you have given	Pinafore II
Good gen'ral monk	Haddon III
Good grand duke, The	Grand Duke I
Good morrow, good lover	Iolanthe I
Good morrow, pretty maids	Gondoliers I
Good mother, good mother	Iolanthe I
Good mother of thy pity say	Ivanhoe II
Good news we bring	Rose II
Good-bye, my native town (by German)	Emerald II
Grave cannot praise Thee, The	Light 1

Great is Olybius, and his mercy great   Antioch 4
Great oak tree, The   Ruddigore II
    "There grew a little flower"
Great Olybius   Antioch 1
Guard by night, A   Chieftain I and Contrab I

Had I the love of such as he   Ruddigore I
Hail, gallant gondolieri   Gondoliers I
Hail! hail! day is dawning   Beauty II
Hail! men-o' warsmen   Pinafore I
Hail, Poetry, thou heav'n-born maid!   Pirates I
Hail the bride of seventeen summers   Ruddigore I
Hail the bridegroom, hail the bride!   Ruddigore I
Hail the bridegroom who advances   Ruddigore I
Hail! the flow'r of England met   Kenilworth
Hail, the valiant fellow   Yeomen II
Hail to our ancient hat   Chieftain I and Contrab I
    "The sacred hat"
Hail to our queen   Chieftain I
Hail to the Lord of Haddon   Haddon I
Hail to the lord of our land   Beauty II
Hallo! hi!   Miller 2
Hand of Fate   Chieftain I and Contrab I
Happily coupled are we   Ruddigore II
Happy are we in our loving frivolity   Sorcerer II
Happy couples, lightly treading   Grand Duke II
Happy day came near, The   Cox
Happy with winged feet   Ivanhoe III
Happy young hearts   Sorcerer I
    "Oh, happy young heart"
Hardly ever run a ship ashore!   Utopia I
Hark! hark! the cannon!   Haddon III
Hark! on the night the clash of falling chains   On Shore
Hark! the distant roll of drums!   Rose I
Hark, the hour of ten is sounding   Trial
Hark! the sound that hails a king   Kenilworth
Hark! those sounds whose accents holy   Legend 3
Hark, what sweet sounds are those   Legend 3

Hark! what was that, sir?	Yeomen II
Hassan, the sultan with his court	Rose II
Hassan! thy pity I entreat	Rose I
Haste thee! haste thee!	Beauty II
Hasten, hasten, O ye spirits!	Legend Prologue
Haughty, humble, coy, or free	Princess II
Have mercy, unrelenting heav'n	Antioch 4
Have pity sir	Contrab II
Have ye heard the brave news	Emerald I
Have you heard of the "Hey diddle diddle"	Rose II
Having been a wicked baronet a week	Ruddigore II
He and she "I know of a youth who loves a little maid"	Ruddigore I
He bought up a great	Haddon I
He bought white ties	Princess II
He can raise you hosts of ghosts	Sorcerer I
He is a little boy of five	Pirates II
He is an Englishman!	Pinafore II
He is! hurray for the orphan boy!	Pirates I
He is telling a terrible story	Pirates I
He isn't at home just now	Grand Duke II
He loves! if in the bygone years	Iolanthe II
He maketh the sun to rise	Light 1
He pardons us, he pardons us	Ruddigore II
He shiver'd and shook	Mikado II
He slapp'd at his chest	Mikado II
He thinks he's won his Josephine	Pinafore I
He who shies at such a prize	Iolanthe II
He, whom his father left to die or live	Ivanhoe II
He will return	Contrab II
He yields! he yields! he answers to our call!	Ruddigore II
He yields his life	Mikado I
Hear me, hear me, if you please	Trial
Heard the dull seagull's mournful cry	Cox
Hearts do not break	Mikado II
Heavy dragoon, The "If you want a receipt"	Patience I
Heavy the sorrow that bows	Pinafore I
Hech, mon! hech, mon!	Haddon III
He'd a couple of shirts	Trial

17

Heighdy! heighdy! misery me	Yeomen I, II
He'll hear no tone	Pinafore II
He'll tell us how he came to be a judge	Trial
He'll trounce them both, upon his oath	Princess I
Henceforth all the crimes that I find	Ruddigore II
Henceforth, Strephon cast away	Iolanthe I
Henceforward, of a verity	Utopia I
Her soul is sweet	Utopia II
Her southern splendour	Ivanhoe II
Her terrible tale	Mikado II
Here a bevy fair of pleasures	Kenilworth
Here am I, too	Legend 3
Here is a case unprecedented	Gondoliers II
Here's a first rate opportunity	Pirates I
Here is a fix unprecendented!	Gondoliers II
Here's a how-de-do!	Mikado II
Here's a man of jollity	Yeomen I
Here's a pretty mess!	Mikado II
Here's a state of things	Mikado II
Here's good luck to Fred'rics ventures	Pirates I
Here's your crowbar	Pirates II
Here, on thy heart	On Shore
Here they come, the couple plighted	Grand Duke I
Here we are, at the risk of our lives	Gondoliers II
Hereupon we're both agreed	Yeomen II
He's got her on the list	Mikado I
Hey, boys! jolly let us be	Chieftain I
Hey willow waly O!	Patience I
Highly respectable gondolier, The	Gondoliers I
"I stole the Prince"	
Him to see--him to view!	Rose I
Him who gave the rose	Beauty I
His eyes should flash	Pinafore I
His foot should stamp	Pinafore I
His Highness we know not	Grand Duke II
His intentions, then he mentions	Utopia I
His lightest word is far preferred	Rose II
His moods you must	Grand Duke II
His nose should pant	Pinafore I
His rightful title	Ruddigore I
His sisters and his cousins	Pinafore I

His spouse, his vows, our rows	Contrab I
Ho, Jolly Jenkin	Ivanhoe II
"The wind blows cold"	
Hoarsely the wind is howling	Haddon II
Hobble, hobble, now we've caught her	Beauty I
Hoity-toity, what's a kiss? (what's an oath?	
who's afraid?)	Haddon II
Hold, monsters!	Pirates I
His object all sublime	Mikado II
Hold! pretty daughter of mine	Pinafore II
Hold, pretty one!	Yeomen II
Homicidal was his madness	Rose II
Honour riches, marriage blessing	Tempest IV
Hooroo, for you	Emerald I
Hop and skip to Fancy's fiddle	Gondoliers I
Hope is for all the world	Ivanhoe I
Hope not at all	Ivanhoe II
Hosanna in the highest!	Light 1
Hosanna to the Son of David	Light 1
Hot cross buns	Miller 1
Hour agone, An	Beauty III
Hour by hour and day by day	Ruddigore I
Hour of gladness is dead, The	Mikado I
Hour of mercy is o'er, The	Antioch 4
Hours creep on apace, The	Pinafore II
House of Peers, The	Iolanthe II
"When Britain really rul'd the waves"	
House of Peers for House of Peris!	Iolanthe II
How beautifully blue the sky	Pirates I
How canst thou know	Ivanhoe III
How dreadful when an innocent heart	Ruddigore II
How fair! how modest!	Utopia I
How many hired servants	Prodigal
How neatly lawyers state a case	Grand Duke I
How oft beneath the far off Syrian skies	Ivanhoe III
How oft when thou wert far beyond	Ivanhoe III
How say you maiden	Yeomen I
How strong is love	Patience
How sweet the moonlight sleeps	Kenilworth
	(scene taken from the
	Merchant of Venice)

How (That) nature always doth contrive	Iolanthe II
How would I play this part	Grand Duke I
Hullo! what's that?	Chieftain I and Contrab I
Humane mikado, A	Mikado II
Humbly beg and humbly sue	Princess I
Hunger, I beg to state	Princess II
Hurrah for the orphan boy	Pirates I
Hurrah, hurrah! I've drawn a king! (an ace!)	Grand Duke I
Hurrah, hurrah! our Ludwig's won	Grand Duke I
Hurrah! now away to the wedding we go	Grand Duke II
Hush! hush! not a word	Pirates II
Hush! not a step	Chieftain I and Contrab I
Hush-a-bye bacon	Cox
Hush'd is the bacon	Cox
Hussar, The	Chieftain I
"From the gay Hussar"	
I am a courtier grave and serious	Gondoliers II
I am a maiden, cold and stately	Princess II
I am a maiden coyly blushing	Princess II
I am a maiden frank and simple	Princess II
I am a pirate king	Pirates I
I am a ruler on the sea	Kenilworth
I am descended from Brian Born	Emerald I
I am grown infirm	Ivanhoe III
I am Loyse from St. Denis	Beauty I
I am so proud	Mikado I
I am the captain of the Pinafore	Pinafore I
I am the Lord Lieutenant	Emerald I
I am the monarch of the sea	Pinafore I, II
I am the ruler of the queen's navee	Pinafore I
I am the very model	Pirates I
I am the very pattern of a modern Major-General	Pirates I
I ask nor wealth nor courtier's praise	Ivanhoe II
I bring thee water	Ivanhoe II
I built upon a rock	Princess II, III
I came with some friends	Chieftain II
I can but tell I knelt and prayed	Beauty I
I can set a braggard quailing	Yeomen I
I cannot, cannot play at love (by German)	Emerald II
I cannot sleep! my fever'd brain	Legend 1

I cannot tell what this love may be	Patience I
I care not how a man be clad	Rose I
I care not if the cup I hold	Rose I
I charge thee	Ivanhoe III
I could love you	Forester II
I could sing if my fervour were mock	Utopia II
I deliver it	Sorcerer I
I do believe that he will come again	Ivanhoe I
I do beseach thee	Ivanhoe II
I do my best to satisfy you all	Pinafore I
I drew a sword of steel	Princess III
I fired each barrel	Contrab II
I fired my pistols	Contrab II
I gave it away	Beauty I
I grew so rich that I was sent	Pinafore I
I have a song to sing	Yeomen I, II
I have discover'd a useful fact	Emerald I
I have dreamed (slept) beneath the water	Kenilworth
I hear the soft note of the echoing	Patience I
I heard him call	Legend 2
I heard one day	Mikado I
I heard the minx remark	Iolanthe I
I know a youth who loves a little maid	Ruddigore I
I know not why I love him so	Sorcerer II
I know our mythic history	Pirates I
I leant upon an oak	Princess III
I love him very dearly	Sorcerer II
I love him with fervour unceasing	Trial
I love thee!	Beauty II
I love you! I love you! (by German)	Emerald II
I love her fondly	Zoo
I mean it truly	Legend 2
I mean to rule the earth	Mikado II
I might have had to live (die)	Yeomen I
I must regain my senses	Sorcerer I
I offered gold in sums untold	Princess III
I often think it's comical	Iolanthe II
I once gave an evening party	Grand Duke II
I once was a very abandon'd person	Ruddigore II
I once was as meek as a newborn lamb	Ruddigore II
I own that that utterance chills me	Grand Duke II

I rejoice that it's decided	Sorcerer II
I said, when I first put it on	Patience I
I see but one thing	Ivanhoe I
I see her tears	Beauty II
I shall lie beneath the flow'rs	Legend 2
I shipp'd d'ye see in a revenue sloop	Ruddigore I
I smoke like a furnace	Trial
I soon found out, beyond all doubt	Pirates I
I stole the prince	Gondoliers I
I think I heard him say	Iolanthe I
I think you ought to recollect	Mikado I
I too had seen a star	Beauty II
I was a stupid nurs'ry maid	Pirates I
I was in the mountains walking	Chieftain II
I was once an exceedingly odd young lady	Ruddigore II
I weigh out tea and sugar	Grand Duke I
I will arise	Prodigal
I will atone for my disdaining!	Gondoliers I
I will pour my spirit	Light 1
I would see a maid (youth)	Beauty II
I'd laugh my rank to scorn	Pinafore I
I'd pit a stap tae jokin'	Haddon II
Ida was a twelve month old	Princess I
If a sudden stroke of Fate	Rose I
If any well-bred youth I knew	Ruddigore I
If anyone anything lacks	Sorcerer I
If death be host	Ivanhoe II
If ever, ever, ever, they get back to Spain	Gondoliers I
If for the love of woman's face	Ivanhoe III
If he ever acts unkindly	Grand Duke I
If he is telling a terrible story	Pirates I
If heart both true and tender	Ruddigore I
If her dress is badly fitting	Grand Duke I
If he's made the best use of his time	Yeomen II
If I allowed my family pride	Mikado I
If I had been so lucky as to have	Ruddigore II
If I should die and you should live	Utopia I
If I to wed the girl am loth	Trial
If I were the youth	Ruddigore I
If in turn he eats another	Grand Duke I
If it is it doesn't matter	Ruddigore II

If ladies' love be worthy prize	Ivanhoe I
If love is a thorn	Patience I
If my speech is unduly refractory	Utopia II
If on Angy I determine	Patience II
If pity you can feel	Pirates I
If Saphir I choose to marry	Patience II
If she come here	Princess I
If she's thy bride, restore her place	Mikado I
If somebody there chanced to be	Ruddigore I
If that is so sing derry down derry!	Mikado II
If the cloak of winter be naught	Beauty III
If the light of love's flickering (lingering) ember	Grand Duke II
If there be pardon in your breast	Patience I
If this indeed be beauty's queen	Beauty I
If this is not exactly right	Patience II
If thou dost see him	Ivanhoe I
If thou dost wrong me	Ivanhoe II
If thou hadst known, O Jerusalem	Light 1
If true her tale thy knell is rung	Mikado I
If we're weak enough to tarry	Iolanthe II
If well his suit has sped	Ruddigore I
If ye be risen with Christ	Light 2
If you and I ourselves ally	Emerald I
If you ask me to advise you	Rose I
If you ask me why	Ruddigore II
If you ask us how we live	Iolanthe I
If you come to grief	Utopia I
If you decide to pocket your pride	Princess II
If you give me your attention	Princess I
If you go in you're sure to win	Iolanthe II
If you or I should tell the truth	Rose II
If you think that, when banded in unity	Utopia II
If you think we are worked by strings	Mikado I
If you value repose and tranquillity	Utopia II
If you vapour vapidly	Yeomen I
If you want a proud foe	Sorcerer I
If you want a receipt	Patience I
If you want to know who we are	Mikado I
If you wish in the world to advance	Ruddigore I
If you wish to appear as an Irish type	Emerald I

If you wish to succeed as a jester	Yeomen II
If you'd climb (cross) the Helicon	Princess II
If your hat you'll be raisin'	Emerald I
If your master is surly	Yeomen II
If you're anxious for to shine	Patience I
I'll never throw dust	Iolanthe I
I'll row and fish	Utopia II
I'll see you to Paris	Chieftain II
I'll storm your walls	Princess II
I'll take heart and make a start	Iolanthe II
I'll tell him that unless	Patience II
I'll tell them what thou wast	Beauty II
I'm a Waterloo House young man	Patience II
I'm Abu-al-Hassan	Rose I
I'm called Little Buttercup	Pinafore I
I'm Captain Corcoran K.C.B.	Utopia I
I'm free! I'm free	Contrab II
I'm much oblig'd to you	Grand Duke II
I'm no saucy minx and giddy	Sorcerer II
I'm pleased with that poetical phrase	Utopia I
I'm rather afraid	Miller 1
I'm such a disagreeable man	Princess I
I'm sure I'm no ascetic	Princess I
I'm telling a terrible story	Pirates I
I'm the sultan's vigilant vizier	Rose I
I'm very good at integral	Pirates I
I'm very much pained to refuse	Iolanthe I
In a contemplative fashion	Gondoliers II
In a doleful train	Patience I, II
In a nest of weeds and nettles	Ruddigore I
In all the childish glee	Grand Duke I
In babyhood on her lap I lay	Iolanthe I
In bygone days I had thy love	Ruddigore II
In days gone by	Sorcerer I
In days of old	Haddon II
In enterprise of martial kind	Gondoliers I
In ev'ry doughty deed	Gondoliers I
In every mental lore	Utopia I
In fact, when I know	Pirates I
In friendship's name	Iolanthe II
In frill and feather	Haddon III

In lazy languor	Utopia I
In lieu of the lily	Haddon I
In life's delight	Legend 6
In other professions	Iolanthe I
In Rama was there a voice heard	Light 1
In return for my (your) own part	Yeomen II
In sailing o'er life's ocean wide	Ruddigore I
In St. Patrick	Emerald II
In serving writs	Pinafore I
In short, in matters vegetable	Pirates I
In short, this happy country	Utopia II
In such a case	Utopia I
In such a night as this	Kenilworth (scene from the Merchant of Venice)
In that case unprecedented	Patience II
In the autumn of our life	Yeomen I
In the first and foremost flight	Gondoliers I
In the heart of my hearts	Rose II
In the moonbeams' magic light	Rose I
In the parliamentary hive	Iolanthe I
In the period Socratic	Grand Duke II
In the springtime	Ruddigore I
In the twilight of our love (words by Hugh Conway) Silver'd is the raven hair (words by W. S. Gilbert)	Patience II
In this cursed place	Ivanhoe II
In towns he makes improvements great	Utopia I
In truth a wonder-working well	Ivanhoe II
In truth I am not blind	Beauty III
In uttering a reprobation	Pinafore II
In vain to us you plead	Iolanthe II
In Westminster Hall I danced a dance	Trial
In your shirt and your sox	Iolanthe II
Incantation "Spirits of earth and air!"	Sorcerer I
Into her heart a canker crept	Haddon III
Into Parliament he shall go!	Iolanthe I
Io Peen (Paean)	Antioch 4
Iolanthe! from thy dark exile thou art summoned	Iolanthe I

Ireland, kick your heels up high	Emerald I
Ireland that's what we'll become wild	Emerald I
Is it but a world of trouble	Mikado I
Is life a boon? (thorn?)	Yeomen I
Is the populace exacting?	Gondoliers II
Is there any one approaching?	Emerald II
Is there aught that shall bind thee	Beauty I
Is there no way of safety?	Ivanhoe II
Is this indeed the king?	Gondoliers II
Isaac, my Jew, my purse of gold	Ivanhoe I
Isle of Rum	Haddon II
It displays a lot of stocking	Grand Duke II
It has no name	Legend 1
It has reached me a lady	Rose II
It is! hurrah for the orphan boy	Pirates I
It is not love	Sorcerer II
"Thou hast the pow'r"	
It is past my comprehension (by German)	Emerald I
It is purely a matter of skill	Yeomen II
It is said a young lady	Rose II
It is sung to the knell	Yeomen I
It is sung to the moon	Yeomen I, II
It is sung with a sigh	Yeomen I
It is sung with the ring	Yeomen I, II
It is the lute	Beauty III
It is the sea	Legend 3
It may not be	Iolanthe II
It may occur to you	Rose I
It means complete indifference	Utopia II
It really is surprising	Utopia II
It typifies unselfishness	Utopia I
It was managed by a job	Trial
It were profanity	Princess III
It's a busy, busy, busy, busy day for thee!	Rose II
It's a hopeless case	Mikado I
It's a horribly harrowing story	Rose II
It's clear that mediaeval art	Patience II
It's clearly understood	Utopia I
It's easy in elegant diction	Pirates I
It's enough to make one shiver	Yeomen II
Its force all men confess	Utopia I

It's Ireland where you'll find him (by German)	Emerald II
It's understood, I think	Utopia I
I've given up all my wild proceedings	Ruddigore II
I've had four tarts	Zoo
I've heard it said	Haddon I
I've jibe (jest) and joke	Yeomen I
I've made a vow	Contrab I
I've wisdom from the East	Yeomen I

Janetta! awake your lover	Miller 1
Joy and sorrow alternate	Rose II
Joyful, joyful! when virginity	Yeomen II
Joyous hour we give thee greeting!	Mikado II
Judge's song, The	Trial
"When I, good friends"	
Judgment! A	Ivanhoe III
Jumping on a steed I gallop'd	Chieftain II

Kind captain, I've important information	Pinafore II
Kind sir, you cannot have the heart	Gondoliers I
King Goodheart	Gondoliers II
"There lived a king, as I've been told"	
King Henry's song	Henry 2
"Youth will needs have dalliance"	
King of autocratic power, A	Utopia I
King Richard, first in rank	Ivanhoe I
Kings of earth stand near, The	Antioch 1
Kiss me, kiss me	Princess II
"Would you know the kind of maid"	
Knightsbridge nursemaids--serving fairies	Utopia I
Know ye all, both great and small	Beauty I

La, la, la, la ... quaff	Utopia I
Ladies fair, I pray you	Haddon I
Lady fair, of lineage high, A	Princess II
Lady Jane's song	Patience II
"Sad is that woman's lot"	
"Silver'd is the raven hair"	
Lady of my love, The	Iolanthe I
Lady of the Lake, The	Kenilworth
"I have slept beneath the water"	
Lady who dyes a chemical yellow, The	Mikado II
Lauda Deum verum!	Legend. Prologue
Laughing boy but yesterday, A	Yeomen I
Laughing low! on tip-toe	Rose II
Law and tradition of Ladrones, The	Chieftain I
Law is the true embodiment, The	Iolanthe I
Leaves in autumn fade and fall	Ruddigore I
Legend of the river, The	Chieftain II
Leonard! (I beg your pardon?)	Yeomen I
Leonard Meryll!	Yeomen I
Leonard Meryll, at his peril	Yeomen I
Leonard, my beloved (loved) one	Yeomen II
Let a satirist numerate a catalogue	Rose II
Let adulation's pleasant breeze	Rose I
Let all your doubts take wing	Utopia I
Let fauns the cymbal ring	Kenilworth
Let hidalgoes be proud of their breed	Contrab II
Let me gaze upon thy face	Zoo
Let me go hence	Beauty II
Let me make it clear to you	Mikado I
Let others seek the peaceful plain	Chieftain I and Contrab I
Let senoras flash brilliant eyes	Contrab II
Let the air with joy be laden	Pinafore II
Let the conqu'ror flush'd with glory	Utopia II
Let the merry cymbals sound	Patience I
Let us dry the ready tear	Mikado II
Let us eat and drink	Prodigal
Let us combine a pose imperious	Gondoliers II
Let us fly to a (the) far off land	Sorcerer I
Let us gaily treat the measure	Pirates I
Let's give three cheers	Pinafore I
Let us grasp the situation	Gondoliers II

Let us lead a life of pleasure	Chieftain I
Let us now go even unto Bethlehem	Light 1
Let us seal this mercantile pact	Utopia I
Lie! my lords, A	Beauty II
Life has put into my hand	Rose I
Life I lead is all I need, The	Rose II
Life is lovely all the year	Ruddigore I
"When the buds are blossoming"	
Light foot upon the dancing green	Ivanhoe III
Like a ghost his vigil keeping	Yeomen II
Like a leaf he shakes with palsy!	Rose II
Like mountain lark	Ivanhoe I
Like summer's bounteous noon	Kenilworth
List and learn, ye dainty roses	Gondoliers I
List, Reginald while I confess	Patience I
Listen! hearken, my lover (by German)	Emerald II
Listen, I solemnly walk'd to the cliff	Cox
Listen, stupid (by German)	Emerald II
Little ball's a flirt, The	Grand Duke II
Little Buttercup	Pinafore I
Little maid of Arcadee	Thespis II
Little wooden soldier, The	Emerald II
"There was once"	
Long live Richard! (Robin!)	Foresters I
Long live the Christian's courage	Antioch 1
Long years ago	Patience I
Look how the floor of heaven	Kenilworth
	(scene from the
	Merchant of Venice)
Look not to thy sword	Arthur
Look on me! in this cursed place	Ivanhoe II
Look, where thy moody father	Ivanhoe III
Look where yonder	Beauty II
Lord, behold, he whom Thou lovest	Light 1
Lord chancellor's song, The	Iolanthe I
"The law is the true embodiment"	
Lord chancelors were cheap as sprats	Gondoliers II
Lord, if Thou hadst been here	Light 1
Lord is nigh unto them, The	Prodigal
Lord is risen, The	Light 2
"Fear not, ye seek Jesus"	

Lord of our chosen race	Ivanhoe II
Lord of the cypress grove	Antioch 1
Lord of the golden day	Antioch 1
Lord of the holy spring	Antioch 1
Lord of the speaking lyre	Antioch 1
Lord of the unerring bow	Antioch 1
Lord, on Thy name I cry	Ivanhoe II
Loudly let the trumpet bray	Iolanthe I
Love breath'd a message	Haddon III
Love feeds on hope	Patience I
Love feeds on many kinds of food	Sorcerer I
Love flew in at the window	Foresters I
Love is a plaintive song	Patience II
Love laid his sleepless head (words by A. C. Swinburne)	Windsor
Love lies not here	Beauty II
Love not the world	Prodigal
Love of arts, The	Chieftain I
Love that no wrong can cure	Patience II
Love, unrequited robs me of my rest	Iolanthe II
Love-sick boy, The "When first my old, old love I knew"	Trial
Lovesick damsel laid, The	Antioch 1
Lower, lower, hover downward	Legend Prologue
Lucky little lady	Iolanthe I
Madam, without the castle walls	Princess II
Madam, your words so wise	Princess II
Magnet and the churn, The "A magnet hung in a hardware shop"	Patience II
Magnet hung in a hardware shop, A	Patience II
Maiden fair to see, A	Pinafore I
Maiden, if e'er in forest free	Ivanhoe III
Maidens and men of Mirlemont Town	Beauty I
Man who would woo, A	Yeomen II
Man will swear and man will storm	Princess II
Many, many people may disbelieve	Emerald I

Many, many years ago	Emerald I
Many years ago I strode	Emerald I
Many years ago these same soft bells	Legend 6
Many years ago when I was young, A	Pinafore II
Marching hither, marching thither	Gondoliers II
Maris stella! from on high	On Shore
Marquis de Mincepie, The	Miller 1
Marvelous illustion! A	Sorcerer I
Master, get Thee out	Light 1
Master, rebuke Thy disciples	Light 1
May all good fortune	Mikado I
May fortune bless you!	Sorcerer I
May it please you, my lud!	Trial
May song, The	Arthur
"Ere upon its snowy bed"	
May we find, as ages run	Exh. Ode
Me receptet Sion	Legend 3
Men of Mirlemont	Beauty II
Merrily, merrily, shall I live now	Tempest V
Merrily ring the luncheon bell!	Princess II
Merry Christmas to you all, A	Miller 3
Merry madrigal, A	Mikado II
"Brightly dawns our wedding day"	
Merry maiden and the tar, The	Pinafore II
"Kind captain, I've important information"	
Merryman and his maid, The	Yeomen I
"I have a song to sing, O!"	
Mighty maiden with a mission	Princess II
Mighty must, The	Princess II
"Come, mighty must!"	
Mikado's song, The	Mikado II
"A more humane Mikado"	
Mille desir me fan soffrir (Barcarole, Serenade)	Venice
(words by F. Rizzelli)	
Mine, mine at last!	Beauty III
Minerva! O hear me	Princess II
Mirage, A	Yeomen I
"Were I thy bride"	
Miya sama, miya sama	Mikado II
Modern major-general, The	Pirates I
"I am the very pattern"	

Monster! dread our fury!	Trial
Moral's safe, The	Grand Duke II
More humane mikado, A	Mikado II
Most intense young man, A	Patience II
Mother, dearest mother	Haddon I
Multiplication is vexation	Emerald I
Musical maidens are we	Rose I
Must we, till then, in prison cell be thrust?	Princess I
My aged employer	Cox
My aid for Ivanhoe	Ivanhoe II
My bill has now been read	Iolanthe II
My boy, you may take it from me	Ruddigore I
My brain it teems	Mikado I
My catalogue is long	Mikado I
My child, I join these congratulations	Sorcerer I
My children I have heard	Beauty I
My dainty bride	Grand Duke II
My eyes are fully open	Ruddigore II
My friends! A Saxon stranger	Emerald I
My gallant crew	Pinafore I
My goodness me! what shall I do?	Grand Duke I
My guests approach	Legend 4
My hand upon it	Cox
My heart says	Ruddigore I
My heart with anguish torn	Pinafore I
My histrionic art	Grand Duke I
My hopes will be blighted I fear	Ruddigore I
My jealousy I can't express	Patience I
My kindly friends, I thank you	Sorcerer I
My life is little	Legend 2
My lord, a suppliant	Iolanthe II
My lord, Grand Duke farewell	Grand Duke I
My lords, it may not be!	Iolanthe I
My love, again to see thee	Chieftain I
My love we'll meet again "He will return"	Contrab II
My love without reflecting	Pirates I
My master is punctual	Cox
My master through has art foresees	Tempest II
My mistress comes	Haddon I
My name is crazy Jacqueline	Beauty I

My name is John Wellington Wells	Sorcerer I
My name it is McCrankie	Haddon II
My natural instinct teaches me	Princess II
My object all sublime	Mikado II
My offer recalling	Grand Duke II
My own, my loved, my beauteous child	Antioch 2
My papa, he keeps three horses	Gondoliers I
My parents were of great gentility	Chieftain I
My prices are low	Haddon I
My Redeemer and my Lord	Legend 2
My son, attend to my words	Prodigal
My soul doth magnify the Lord	Light 1
My subjects all	Utopia I
My task is done	Ivanhoe II
Mystic poet, hear our prayer	Patience I

Naught shall divide (by German)	Emerald II
Nay, father dear	Haddon I
Nay, grieve not in a little while	Beauty II
Nay, nay, in pity hear me!	Beauty II
Nay, tempt me not	Iolanthe I
Nay, wert thou more	Beauty II
'Neath my lattice through the night	Rose I
'Neath this blow	Iolanthe I
Neither that grandee from the Spanish shore	Gondoliers I
Nel ciel seren di stelle (Barcarole, Serenade) (words by F. Rizzelli)	Venice
Never mind the why and wherefore (Bell trio)	Pinafore II
Nice dilemma we have here, A	Trial
Night and the day are one, The	Beauty I
Night has spread her fall once more	Yeomen II
Night is calm and cloudless, The	Legend 3
Night will come soon	Haddon I
Night winds sigh alone "The tinkling sheepbell knells the parting day"	Chieftain I
Nightingale sigh'd, The	Pinafore I

Nightingale's song, The	Pinafore I
"The nightingale sighed"	
Nightmare, A	Iolanthe II
"When you're lying awake"	
No chastening	Prodigal
No Englishman unmov'd	Pirates II
No grace is in grief	Haddon I
No! if there be pardon	Patience I
No, no! let the bygone go by!	Grand Duke II
No (For) nobody can know, to a million or so	Utopia I
No possible doubt whatever	Gondoliers I
No thanks, my boy	Miller 1
No way but through the gates of death	Ivanhoe II
No word for Ivanhoe	Ivanhoe I
No word of thine--no stern command	Princess II
No young giddy thoughtless maiden	Sorcerer II
Noble lord who rules the state	Gondoliers I
Nocte surgentis	Legend Prologue
Noel	12 Carols
Noisome hags of night	Sorcerer I
None but the chief e'er saw	Contrab I
None shall part us	Iolanthe I
None so cunning as he	Sorcerer I
None so knowing as he	Sorcerer I
Nor violet, lily	Haddon I
Not a moment's hesitation	Yeomen II
Not a word--you did deceive me (her)	Iolanthe I
Not long ago	Cox
Not one step further!	Legend 4
Not so, not so, my doubting heart (by German)	Emerald I
Not thus did Judah's warriors	Ivanhoe III
Nothing venture, nothing win	Iolanthe II
Now a gavotte perform	Gondoliers II
Now among the bricks	Rose II
Now as a fairy tale always ends	Miller 3
Now away to the wedding we go	Grand Duke II
Now be aisy wid taisin'	Emerald I
Now bridegroom and bride	Grand Duke II
Now by my own sword	Ivanhoe II
Now coals is coals	Cox

Now don't be foolish dear	Grand Duke I
Now ev'ry Irish boy	Emerald I
Now for an attitude	Gondoliers II
Now for the pirates' lair!	Pirates II
Now (Then) Frederic, let your escort lion-hearted	Pirates II
Now give three cheers	Pinafore, I, II
Now Glory to God who breaks	Antioch 4
Now hearken to my strict command	Princess I
Now here's a first rate opportunity	Pirates I
Now he's eighty-three	Emerald I
Now, how is this, and what is this?	Emerald I
Now I feel just as sure	Mikado II
Now if Brian Boru were about	Emerald I
Now if God will	Ivanhoe III
Now is not this ridiculous?	Patience I
Now isn't that beautiful	Haddon I
Now Julia, come, consider it	Grand Duke II
Now, jurymen, hear my advice	Trial
Now landsmen all	Pinafore I
Now let the loyal lieges gather round	Gondoliers II
Now listen, pray, to me	Iolanthe I
Now, Marco dear, my wishes hear	Gondoliers I
Now, nay, fair flower of Palestine	Ivanhoe II
Now philosophy may frown	Rose II
Now, pray, what is the cause	Gondoliers I
Now shrivelled hags, with poison bags	Sorcerer I
Now step lightly	Haddon II
Now take a card, and gaily sing	Grand Duke I
Now take, for example, my case	Ruddigore I
Now tell us, we pray you	Patience I
Now that gold of mine	Rose I
Now that little wooden soldier	Emerald II
Now the king is home again	Foresters IV
Now the passage to a drawing room (by German)	Emerald II
Now, this is the song of the Devonshire men (by German)	Emerald I
Now though you'd have said	Mikado II
Now to the banquet we press	Sorcerer I, II
Now to the other extreme	Gondoliers II
Now what can that have been	Yeomen II

Now what could I	Yeomen II
Now what is this, and what is that	Pirates II
Now, with the first note	Miller 3
Now wouldn't you like to rule the roost?	Princess II
Now ye know, ye dainty roses	Gondoliers I

O awful depth below the castle wall	Ivanhoe II
O bliss! O rapture!	Pinafore II
O donde esta la criada?	Chieftain II
O fool, that fleest my hallowed joys	Mikado I
O gentlemen, listen I pray	Trial
O gladsome light of the Father immortal	Legend 2
O God of Israel	Ivanhoe III
O golden key	Rose I
O, happy young heart	Sorcerer I
O ladies, what assails you?	Rose I
O lady, do not fail	Rose I
O listen to a mother's fond appeal!	Iolanthe II
O love that holds the world	Ivanhoe III
O luckless hour! O dreadful day!	Rose I
O maiden rich	Utopia I
O make way for the wise men!	Utopia I
O moon, art thou clad in silver mail	Ivanhoe I
O moralists all	Gondoliers II
O my darling, O my pet	Gondoliers I
O ni! bikuri shakuri to!	Mikado I
O papa! though, papa	Emerald I
O perjured lover, atone, atone	Trial
O pure in heart	Legend 4
O rapture, when alone together	Gondoliers I
O royal rex, my blameless sex	Utopia I
O setting sun (by German)	Emerald I
O that men would praise the Lord	Prodigal
O that thou hadst hearkened	Prodigal
O 'twixt prudence	Rose I
O, we cannot for around it	Legend Prologue
O, we cannot, the apostles (archangel)	Legend Prologue

36

O wind that awakest	Ivanhoe I
Observe his flame	Mikado II
Observe this dance	Utopia I
Och! the spalpeen! let him drown! (by German)	Emerald II
Ode: see Index II	
O'er Mirlemont City the banners are flying	Beauty III
O'er the season vernal	Trial
Of a tyrant polite	Utopia I
Of all the young ladies I know	Iolanthe I
Of birth and position he's plenty	Iolanthe I
Of happiness the very pith	Gondoliers II
Of legal knowledge I acquired such a grip	Pinafore I
Of life, alas! his leave he's taking	Pinafore I
Of overpow'ring high degree	Rose II
Of Torquilstone!	Ivanhoe I
Of viceroys though we've had	Emerald I
Oh, a monarch who boasts	Grand Duke I
Oh, a private buffoon	Yeomen II
Oh, admirable art!	Utopia I
Oh, agony, rage, despair	Sorcerer II
Oh, better far to live and die	Pirates I
Oh, bitter joy!	Sorcerer II
Oh, bury, bury--let the grave close	Gondoliers I
Oh! chancellor unwary	Iolanthe I
Oh, dainty toilet!	Princess I
Oh, day of terror!	Yeomen II
Oh, don't the days seem lank	Princess II, III
Oh! dry the glist'ning tear	Pirates II
Oh! false one, you have deceived me!	Pirates I
Oh, fit the arrows of respect	Rose I
Oh fool that fleest my hallowed joys!	Mikado I
Oh, foolish fay!	Iolanthe II
Oh, forestways are dark enow	Ivanhoe III
Oh, Fortune, to my aching heart be kind	Patience I
Oh! go search the world	Utopia II
Oh, goddess wise	Princess II
Oh, happy day, with joyous glee	Pirates I
Oh, happy the blossoms (flowers, lily)	Ruddigore I
Oh, happy young heart	Sorcerer I
Oh, hard to please	Gondoliers II
Oh, have you met a man in debt	Emerald II

37

Oh, hear me, Olybius	Antioch 3
Oh, heart's desire	Haddon II
Oh, here is love and here is truth	Pirates II
Oh, his rule will be merry	Grand Duke I
Oh, I have wrought much evil	Sorcerer II
Oh, I love the jolly rattle	Princess III
Oh, I was like that when a lad	Trial
Oh! I would be an outlaw bold	Ivanhoe III
Oh innocent, happy, though poor!	Ruddigore I
Oh, is there not one maiden breast	Pirates I
Oh, it's simply uncanny	Grand Duke I
Oh Jehovah, guard oh guard me	Ivanhoe III
Oh joy! oh joy! the charm works well	Sorcerer II
Oh joy, oh rapture unforseen!	Pinafore I, II
Oh! joy, our chief is sav'd	Princess II
Oh joy unbounded	Trial
Oh joy! when two glowing young hearts	Grand Duke I
Oh, joyous boon!	Sorcerer II
Oh, kiss me!	Princess II
Oh list while we a love confess	Patience I
Oh, listen to me dear	Grand Duke I
Oh, listen to the plaintiff's case	Trial
Oh, living I come tell me why	Mikado II
Oh love, true love!	Sorcerer I
Oh, maiden rich	Utopia I
Oh, maids of high and low degree	Utopia I
Oh, many a man, in friendship's name	Iolanthe II
Oh, marvelous illusion	Sorcerer I
Oh, may we copy all her maxims wise	Utopia II
Oh! men of dark and dismal fate	Pirates I
Oh, mercy, thou whose smile	Yeomen I
Oh, mistress dear, tonight and here	Haddon II
Oh, my brain is whirling	Chieftain II
Oh, my joy, my pride	Utopia I
Oh! my name is John Wellington Wells	Sorcerer I
Oh, my voice is sad and low	Sorcerer II
Oh, never, never, never	Trial
Oh, never shall I forget the cry	Mikado II
Oh, philosophers may sing	Gondoliers II
Oh rapture! away to the parson we go	Ruddigore II
Oh rapture unrestrained	Utopia II

Oh rapture! when alone together	Gondoliers I
Oh, Sergeant Meryll, is it true--	Yeomen I
Oh, setting sun (by German)	Emerald I
Oh, shameless one! Oh boldfaced thing!	Patience I
Oh, shameless one, tremble!	Iolanthe I
Oh, sir, he's such a handsome youth	Haddon III
Oh, stop, do stop	Miller 3
Oh, sweet surprise	Utopia II
Oh, tell me what is a maid to say?	Haddon I
Oh, the age in which we're living (by German)	Emerald II
Oh, the doing and undoing	Yeomen II
Oh, the happy days of doing!	Yeomen II
Oh! the hours are gold	Utopia I
Oh, the man who can drive (rule)	Grand Duke I
Oh, the rapture unrestrained	Utopia II
Oh, the skies are blue above	Utopia II
Oh, this is absurd	Cox
Oh, 'tis a glorious thing	Gondoliers I
Oh, turn thine eyes away	Beauty I
Oh, weak might be!	Princess II
Oh, what is love?	Rose II
Oh, what is the matter	Sorcerer II
Oh why am I moody and sad?	Ruddigore I
Oh will you swear by yonder skies	Trial
Oh willow, titwillow	Mikado II
Oh, woe is me	Yeomen I
Oh, would some demon power	Utopia II
Oh, wretched the debtor	Ruddigore I
Oh! yield at once	Princess II
Oh! you very, very plain old man	Sorcerer II
Oh, Zara!	Utopia II
Old Athens let's (we'll) exhume	Grand Duke I
Old Xeres we'll drink manzanilla	Gondoliers II
On a tree by a river	Mikado II
On every other point than this	Princess II
On fire that glows	Iolanthe II
On such a night as this	Kenilworth (scene from the Merchant of Venice)
On such eyes as maidens cherish	Patience II
On sweet urbanity	Princess I
On the day when I was wedded	Gondoliers II
On the heights of Glantaun	Emerald I

On this subject we pray you	Mikado I
On with the sports, I say!	Ivanhoe I
Once again the vows are broken	Iolanthe II
Once more gondolieri	Gondoliers II
Once, on the village green	Ruddigore I
One lovely summer day	Chieftain II
One morn when I had finish'd	Cox
One remains, and if that be true	Emerald I
Only roses!	Ruddigore I
"To a garden full of posies"	
Only the nightwind sighs alone	Chieftain I and Contrab I
"The tinkling sheepbell knells"	
Onward and onward on the highway	Legend 3
Onward! with the night wind onward	Legend
	Prologue
Opoponex! Eloia!	Grand Duke II
Or he or I must die!	Sorcerer II
Or your own shillelagh	Emerald I
Our city we have beautiful	Utopia II
Our disrespectful sneers	Iolanthe II
Our duty, if we're wise	Grand Duke I
Our duty is to spy	Utopia I
Our great mikado, virtuous man	Mikado I
Our heads we bow	Haddon III
Our holy order grows	Ivanhoe II
Our interests we would not press	Princess II
Our lordly style	Iolanthe I
Our mortal race is never blest	Utopia I
Our peerage we've remodell'd	Utopia II
Our queen may let such bodings pass	Kenilworth
Our soldiers very seldom cry	Patience I
Our tale is told	Rose II
Outside a mob of people expectant hums	Rose II
Over field, and farm, and forest	Legend
	Prologue
Over the bright blue sea	Pinafore I
Over the ripening peach	Ruddigore I
Over the roof, and over the wall	Sapphire

Pack up at once and off we go	Grand Duke I
Pain, trouble and care	Sorcerer I
Painted emblems of a race	Ruddigore II
Paradox, a paradox, a most ingenious, A	Pirates II
Pastime with good company (words by Henry VIII)	Henry 2
Pattern to professors of monarchical autonomy, A	Grand Duke I
Peace be upon this house!	Rose I
Peace, idle man!	Ivanhoe II
Periphrastic methods spurning	Grand Duke II
Philosophic pill, The	Yeomen I
"I've wisdom from the East"	
Phoebus Apollo	Antioch 1
Pierced thro' each scaly fold	Antioch 1
Pinch him and burn him	Windsor
Pink cheek, that rulest	Mikado I
Place for the queen!	Kenilworth
Plantagenesta! hail the lords of land and sea	Ivanhoe I
Pleasant occupation, A	Iolanthe I
Pluck of Lord Nelson, The	Patience I
Policeman's lot, The	Pirates II
"When a felon's not engaged"	
Poor little maid (man)	Ruddigore I
Poor wandering ones!	Pirates II
Poor wand'ring one	Pirates I
Pour, O king, (oh pour) the pirate sherry	Pirates I
P'raps if you address the lady	Princess I
Pray observe the magnanimity	Pirates I
Pray, what authors should she read	Princess II
Pray you, tell us, if you can	Princess II
Preach me no more, daughter of Sirach!	Ivanhoe II
Prepare for sad surprises!	Sorcerer I
Pretty brook, thy dream is over	Pirates II
Pretty Lisa, fair and tasty	Grand Duke I
Pretty little flower	Ruddigore II
"There grew a little flower"	
Prince of Monte Carlo, The	Grand Duke II
Printer, printer, take a hinter	Cox
Pris'ner comes to meet his doom, The	Yeomen I
Prithee, pretty maiden	Patience I

Prompted by a keen desire	Ruddigore II
Proper pride	Mikado II
"The sun, whose rays are all ablaze"	
Prophecy came true, The	Ruddigore I
Proud lady, have your way	Pinafore I
Pull ashore, in fashion steady	Pinafore II
Purge your nostrums	Legend 1

Quaff the nectar	Utopia I
Queen of the garden bloom'd a rose	Haddon III
Queen of the roses	Haddon III
Question, gentlemen, The	Trial
Quite (Then) reassured, I let him know	Grand Duke I

Rapture, rapture! When love's votary	Yeomen II
Rataplan (Bouncer's Song)	
"Yes! yes! in those merry days"	Cox
"There was once a little soldier"	Emerald II
Recipe, A	Gondoliers II
"Take a pair of sparkling eyes"	
Red of the rosebud	Haddon I
Refrain, audacious tar	Pinafore II
Refrain thy voice from weeping	Light 1
Regular royal queen, A	Gondoliers I
Release me	Beauty II
Rend the air with wailing	Princess II
Rendering good for ill	Patience II
Replying, we sing as one individual	Gondoliers I
Rest, rest, O give me rest and peace	Legend 1
Ribbons to sell	Haddon I
Rich attorney he jumped with joy, The	Trial
Rich attorney was good as his word, The	Trial
Riches and rank that you befall, The	Iolanthe I
Ring forth, ye bells	Sorcerer I
Ring the merry bells on board ship	Pinafore II

Rise, and go forth with us who seek the Grail	Arthur
Rise, holy Palmer!	Ivanhoe I
Rising early in the morning	Gondoliers II
River, river, little river	Pirates II
River! the river!, The	Chieftain II
Rollicking band of pirates we, A	Pirates II
Rose, all glowing	Ruddigore I
Rose of Sharon, The	Ivanhoe I
Rover's apology, The	Trial
"O gentlemen, listen, I pray"	
Rowena!	Ivanhoe I
Royal prince was by the king entrusted, The	Gondoliers II
Rum-tum-tum of the military drum, The	Princess I
Rupert Murgatroyd	Ruddigore I

Sacred hat, The	Chieftain I & Contrab I
Sacrifices of God, The	Prodigal
Sad is that woman's lot	Patience II
Sad is the hour when sets the sun	Pinafore I
Safe in her island home	Beauty II
Said I not unto thee	Light 1
Said I to myself, said I	Iolanthe I
"When I went to the bar"	
Said she "He loved me never"	Ruddigore II
Sancho, surnamed "The Badger"	Chieftain I
Sans Souci	Patience I
"I cannot tell what this love may be"	
Saxon heart is bold for right	Ivanhoe I
School girls we, eighteen and under	Mikado I
Scotch dance	Haddon III
Screw may twist, The	Yeomen I
Search throughout the panorama	Princess I
Second to none	Ivanhoe I
See how the fates their gift allot	Mikado II
See my interesting client	Trial
See, they sign, without a quaver	Sorcerer I
Sentry's song, The	Iolanthe II
"When all night long"	

44

Sing hey, the jolly jinks	Grand Duke I
Sing "Hey to you good-day to you"	Patience II
Sing high, sing low, wherever they go	Gondoliers I
Sing, hoity toity! Sorry for some	Princess II
Sing me your song	Yeomen I
Sink and scatter, clouds of war	On Shore
Sir, I thank you	Sorcerer I
Sir Joseph's barge is seen	Pinafore I
"We sail the ocean blue"	
Sir Marmaduke	Sorcerer I
Sir Rupert Murgatroyd	Ruddigore I
Sir, you are sad	Pinafore I
Sit with downcast eye	Mikado II
Sixes	Cox
Skylark's trill, The	Yeomen I
Sleep, gentle bacon	Cox
Sleep, great queen!	Kenilworth
Sleep! oh, sleep! 'til night outworn (Funeral	
march)	Arthur
Slowly, slowly up the wall	Legend 2
Small street Arab, The	Rose II
Small titles and orders for mayors	Gondoliers II
Smiling summer beams upon her	Ruddigore I
So all is lost for ever!	Beauty III
So amiable I've grown	Yeomen I
So bumpers--aye, ever-so-many	Grand Duke II
So care now departs	Contrab I
So down with them	Utopia II
So ends my dream	Grand Duke II
So go to him and say to him	Patience II
So good-bye, cachucha	Gondoliers II
So here we are	Gondoliers II
So I came to town	Rose I
So I waited years to find a lady	Emerald I
So in spite of all temptation	Mikado I
So it really doesn't matter	Ruddigore II
So please you, sir, we much regret	Mikado I
So spectre appalling	Grand Duke II
So the clock that strikes	Rose II
So we up with our helm	Ruddigore I
Society has quite forsaken	Utopia II

Soft and sadly, sea-wind, swell	On Shore
Softly sighing to the river	Pirates II
Solatium	Trial
"Comes the broken flower"	
Soldiers of our queen, The	Patience I
Soldiers, prepare, to leave your bivouacs	Emerald I
Some kind of charm you seem to find	Gondoliers I
Some maids have played at love (by German)	Emerald II
Some misfortune evidently	Princess I
Some seven men form an association	Utopia I
Some years ago	Princess II
Something yet may advertise you	Rose I
Song of birds, The	Utopia I
Song of peace	On Shore
"Sink and scatter"	
Sons of the tillage (village), The	Ruddigore I
Soon as we may off and away	Iolanthe II
Sorcere's song, The	Sorcerer I
"My name is John Wellington Wells"	
Sorry her lot who loves too well	Pinafore I
Sound the trumpet, roll the drums	Emerald I
South blows the wind	Beauty II
Speculation	Mikado I
"Comes a train of little ladies"	
Spirit of the Lord is upon me, The	Light 1
Spirit, who movest ev'rywhere	Ivanhoé II
Spring and summer pleasure you	Ruddigore I
Spring is green	Ruddigore I
Spring is hope	Ruddigore I
Sprites of earth and air!	Sorcerer I
Spurn not the nobly born	Iolanthe I
Stay, Bouncer, stay!	Cox
Stay, Fred'ric, stay!	Pirates II
Stay, we implore you	Patience I
Stay, we must not lose our senses	Pirates I
Stern conviction's o'er him stealing	Pinafore II
Still brooding on their mad infatuation	Patience I
Still, I was a tiny prince	Princess I
Stop, ladies, pray! a man	Pirates I
Story teller am I, A	Rose I
Strange adventure! maiden wedded	Yeomen II

Strange lodging this for England's king	Ivanhoe II
Strange proposal you reveal, A	Yeomen I
Strange the views some people hold	Grand Duke I
Strephon's member of Parliament	Iolanthe II
String the lyre and fill the cup	Gondoliers I
Stupendous when we rouse ourselves	Utopia I
Subjected to your heavenly gaze	Utopia I
Submit to fate	Gondoliers I
Such a disagreeable man	Princess I
"If you give"	
Such a very, very pretty wedding	Grand Duke I
Such, at least, is the tale	Utopia II
Such escort duty	Utopia I
Such is my best	Chieftain I
Such love is like the ray	Sorcerer II
Suicidal was our sadness	Rose I
Suicide's grave, The	Mikado II
"On a tree by a river"	
Suitor approached, A	Chieftain I
Sultan's executioner, The	Rose I
Sultan is Hassan, The	Rose I
Sun's in the sky, The	Haddon I
Sun, whose rays are all ablaze, The	Mikado II
Sunbeam! The priest keeps saying	Rose I
Sunlight takes the place of shade	Gondoliers I
Suppose--I say, suppose	Rose II
Supreme content and happiness	Utopia I
Swear to be mine	Ivanhoe III
Sweet and low	Utopia II
Sweet is the air	Legend 3
Sweet maid, heav'n too lies afar	Beauty I
Sweet Margarita, give me the hand	Antioch 3
Sweetheart, betake thyself to bed	Emerald I
Sweetly the morn doth break	Haddon I
Swiftly fled each honeyed hour	Trial
Sylvans, The	Kenilworth
"Let fauns the cymbal ring"	

Take a pair of sparkling eyes	Gondoliers II
Take a pretty little cot	Gondoliers II
Take a tipsy lout	Iolanthe II
Take a wretched thief	Iolanthe II
Take Bagdad and Bonn	Chieftain II
Take care of him	Grand Duke II
Take heart, no danger lowers	Pirates I
Take my advice--when deep in debt	Grand Duke II
Take my council, happy man	Gondoliers II
Take thou these jewels	Ivanhoe II
Taken from the county jail	Mikado I
Tale so free, A	Gondoliers I
Tall snobs, small snobs	Grand Duke I
Tangled skein, The	Gondoliers I
"Try we lifelong, we can never"	
Tantantarara	Utopia I
	Iolanthe I
Taradiddle idyll	Rose II
Taradiddle, taradiddle, tol lol lay	Iolanthe I
Tarantara	Pirates II
Taste for drink combined with gout	Gondoliers I
Tell a tale of cock and bull	Yeomen II
Tell ye the daughter of Zion	Light 1
Temple stands, The	Ivanhoe III
Temptation, oh, temptation	Yeomen I
Ten minutes since I met a chap	Grand Duke I
Ten minutes since my heart said "white"	Ruddigore I
Ten years later	Utopia I
Tenor, all singers above, A	Utopia II
Thank you for your gallant (kindly) proffer	Sorcerer II
Thank you, gallant gondolieri	Gondoliers I
That (And) a victim must be found	Mikado I
That both these maids	Grand Duke I
That king, although no one denies	Gondoliers II
That our voices are clear as a bell	Rose I
That seems a reasonable proposition	Trial
That she is reeling	Trial
That simple weed--he did indeed	Rose II
That two are two	Cox
That very knowing	Gondoliers I
That was true love	Legend 6

That we're soldiers no doubt you will guess	Emerald I
That's true--we South Pacific viviparians	Utopia I
Their courage high, you may defy	Emerald I
Their fathers fought at Ramillies	Emerald I
Their lives you bear away!	On Shore
Then a glance may be timid	Yeomen II
Then a sentimental passion	Patience I
Then away they (we) go	Gondoliers I
Then (Now), Frederic, let your escort	Pirates II
Then give three cheers	Pinafore I
Then goodbye to your sisters	Pinafore II
Then hail, O king of a golden land	Gondoliers II
Then hail! O king whichever you may be	Gondoliers I
Then ho, jolly Jenkin	Ivanhoe II
Then I can write a washing bill	Pirates I
Then I may sing and play?	Utopia II
Then it pass'd to a miser	Beauty 5
Then jump for joy	Princess II
Then let the throng our joy advance	Mikado I, II
Then let us modestly merry	Grand Duke I
Then let's rejoice with loud fa la-	Iolanthe II
Then man the capstan	Mikado I
Then, marry, come here and dance with me	Beauty I
Then one of us will be a queen	Gondoliers I
Then our capt'n he up and he says	Ruddigore I
Then (Quite) reassur'd, I let him know	Grand Duke
Then scatter the cards	Beauty II
Then tell us	Beauty I
Then the air with love is laiden	Gondoliers I
There are cases	Chieftain II
There are women I've known	Rose II
There grew a little flower	Ruddigore II
There he stands, that lord ye knew	Beauty II
There is beauty in the bellow	Mikado II
There is joy in the presence of the angels of God	Prodigal
There is no land like England	Foresters II
There lived a king, as I've been told	Gondoliers II
There shall come forth a rod	Light 1
There was a time forever gone	Gondoliers I
There was once a little soldier	Emerald II

There was once a small street Arab	Rose II
There were shepherds	Light 1
There's a little group of isles	Utopia II
There's no one by	Haddon II
There's no one I'm certain	Chieftain II
There's the nigger serenader	Mikado I
There's vulgar imitation (by German)	Emerald II
These are the phenomena	Princess II
These brassets, truth to tell	Princess III
These children whom you see	Pirates I
They alas, are only two	Gondoliers I
They are done, dear Elsie	Legend 6
They are men of might, ha! ha!	Princess I
They are not exaggerated	Yeomen I
They are too strong	Ivanhoe I
They chain not Christian souls	On Shore
They do not speak	Grand Duke II
They fled to the mountain	Chieftain I
They intend to send a wire	Princess II
They mock at him	Princess II
They never would be missed	Mikado I
They shall (will) both go on requesting	Gondoliers II
They then proceed to trade	Utopia I
They travel through France	Chieftain II
They'll none of 'em be missed!	Mikado I
"As some day it may happen"	
They're actually sneering at us	Patience I
Thine is the power	Sorcerer II
Things are seldom what they seem	Pinafore II
Thinking thickly	Rose I
This ceremonial our wish displays	Utopia II
This county councillor acclaim	Utopia I
This haughty youth	Mikado II
This heart of mine	Yeomen I
This helmet I suppose	Princess II, III
This holy relic	Ivanhoe I
This is my joy-day unalloyed	Yeomen II
"'Tis said that joy is full perfection"	
This is our duty plain	Princess III
This is the consequence	Pinafore II
This life of ours is a wild aeolian harp	Legend 3

This little flask contains	Legend 1
This polite attention	Gondoliers II
This sport he much enjoyed	Ruddigore I
This statement we receive	Gondoliers II
This step to use	Utopia I
This stern degree you'll understand	Mikado I
This the autumn of our life	Yeomen I
This tight fitting cuirass	Princess III
This very night	Pinafore II
Tho' in body and in mind	Pirates II
Tho' obedience is strong, curiosity's stronger	Gondoliers II
Tho' our hearts she's badly bruising	Iolanthe I
Tho' p'rhaps I may incur your blame "In friendship's name"	Iolanthe II
Tho' vow'd to the habit of sloth	Rose I
Thorns are in my shoes, The	Miller 2
Those (We're) pressing prevailers	Gondoliers II
Those (We're) ready as witness	Gondoliers II
Thou art his father	Ivanhoe II
Thou askest what is a maid to say	Haddon I
Thou hast the pow'r	Sorcerer II
Thou Jewish girl, who are condemned to die	Ivanhoe III
Thou know'st the story of her ring	Legend 6
Thou mountest heav'n's blue steep	Antioch 1
Thou, O Lord, art our Father	Prodigal
Thou the dead hero's name	Antioch 1
Thou the stream and I the willow (tree and I the flower)	Iolanthe I
Thou wilt not see it	Legend 2
Though a doctor of divinity	Pirates I
Though as a general rule we know	Iolanthe II
Though as a gen'l rule of life	Yeomen I
Though her (my) station	Iolanthe I
Though I am but a girl	Princess II
Though my book I seem to scan	Patience I
Though obedience is strong, curiosity's stronger	Gondoliers II
Though she should dance, till dow' of day	Beauty II
Though so excellently wise	Patience I
Though tear and longdrawn sigh	Yeomen I
Though the hours are surely creeping	Mikado II
Though the views of the house	Iolanthe I

Though to marry you	Patience I
Though with roses we crown thee today	Beauty I
Though your head it may rack	Yeomen II
Threatened cloud has passed away, The	Mikado I, II
Three ages, The	Utopia I
"First you're born"	
Three little girls (maids) from school are we	Mikado I
Three years ago	Cox
Through ev'ry vein I feel again	Legend 1
Through my book I seem to scan	Patience I
Through tear and long drawn sigh	Yeomen I
Throughout the day	Rose I
Thus our courage, all untarnished	Princess III
Thy love is but a flow'r	Sorcerer II
Thy love is more to me	Ivanhoe III
Till into one of the blue lakes	Legend 6
Time, my course with judgement shaping	Yeomen I
Time sped, and when at the end of a year	Gondoliers I
Time, the avenger	Haddon II
Time was, Sir Knight, thou spurn'd me from thy gate	Haddon III
Time was, when love and I were well-acquainted	Sorcerer I
Time will soften ev'ry blow	Rose I
Tinkling sheepbell knells, The	Chieftain I
'Tis a difficult case	Chieftain II
'Tis a peewit	Chieftain I
'Tis but the pause before the onset	Ivanhoe III
'Tis done! I am a bride	Yeomen I
'Tis ever thus	Yeomen I
'Tis said that joy in full perfection	Yeomen II
'Tis the midwatch of night	On Shore
'Tis very hard to choose	Chieftain I
Titwillow	Mikado II
"On a tree by a river"	
To a garden full of posies	Ruddigore I
To a land where the fay	Foresters II
To a word of warning hark	Haddon III
To all of this we make reply	Trial
To compliments inflated	Princess I
To lay aloft in a howling breeze	Mikado I

To love for money all the world is prone	Sorcerer I
To men of grosser clay	Gondoliers I
To say she is his mother	Iolanthe I
To sing my own praises	Rose I
To sit in solemn silence	Mikado I
To sleep! to sleep!	Foresters I
"To Spain," said my husband	Chieftain II
To the queen we will appeal	Chieftain I
To thine own heart be true	Haddon I, III
To thy fraternal care	Yeomen I
To yield at once to such a foe	Princess II
To you I give my heart	Iolanthe I
Today, it is a festal time (the festal day)	Haddon I
Today we meet	Princess I
Tol the riddle lol!	Grand Duke II
Tonight he dies!	Pirates II
Too late--too late it may not be!	Sorcerer I
Tormented with the anguish dread	Pirates II
Tossing in a manner frightful	Gondoliers II
Toujours si gaie	Chieftain II
Towards the empyrean heights	Princess II
Tower tomb	Yeomen II
Tower warders, under orders	Yeomen I
Tra, la, la, la	Grand Duke II
Tra la, tra la	Gondoliers I
	Mikado II
Tramps and scamps and halt and blind	Rose I
Tripping hither, tripping thither	Iolanthe I
True diffidence	Ruddigore I
"My boy, you may take it from me"	
True love must be single-hearted	Patience I
Truly I was to be pitied	Yeomen I
Trust in the Lord	Prodigal
Try we life-long, we can never	Gondoliers I
Tune your lay	Emerald II
Turn, oh turn in this direction	Patience II
'Twas a dear little dormouse	Haddon I
'Twas in Hyde Park beside the row	Emerald II
'Twas not enough thy youth should waste	Beauty II
Twenty lovesick maidens we	Patience I
Twenty years ago	Princess I

53

Two happy gods	Chieftain II
Two is company	Emerald I
Two kings, of undue pride bereft	Gondoliers II
Two there are for whom, in duty	Gondoliers I

Uhlalica	Utopia I
Until quite plain	Utopia I
Up and down, and in and out	Yeomen II
Up in the sky	Iolanthe II
Upon our sea-girt land	Utopia II
Upon thy breast	Yeomen I
Urbs coelestis	Legend 3
Usher's charge, The	Trial
"Now, jurymen, hear my advice"	

Vainly on thy bended knee	Beauty I
Venetian serenade	Venice
"Nel ciel seren di stelle"	
"Mille desir mi fan soffrir"	
Very susceptible chancellor, A	Iolanthe I
Vicar's song, The	Sorcerer I
"Time was, when love and I"	
Virgin, who lovest the poor	Legend 4
Visions of Brighton and back	Cox
Viva! a bias to disclose	Gondoliers I
Viva! his argument is strong	Gondoliers I
Vow you make you must not break, A	Princess II

Wake, gentle maiden	Contrab II
Wake, then, awake!	Chieftain II
Walls and fences scaling	Princess II
Wand'ring minstrel, A	Mikado I

Wanted, a chieftain	Chieftain I
Warders are we (ye)	Yeomen II
Warrior Earl of Allendale, The	Foresters I
Was hael!	Ivanhoe I, II
Wave at her bows, The	On Shore
We are alone	Legend 6
We are blind, and we would see	Princess II
We are dainty little fairies	Iolanthe I
We are dreaming	Beauty II
We are peers of highest station	Iolanthe I
We are ready as witness	Gondoliers II
We are rigged out in magnificent array	Grand Duke II
We are warriors three	Princess I
We be scar'd with song and shout	Foresters II
We believe that Thou shalt come	F. Te Deum
We care so much for a king	Foresters III
We do not heed their dismal sound	Mikado I
We elop'd, and he said	Chieftain I
We fear no rude rebuff	Utopia I
We have come to invade	Rose I
We have thought the matter out	Haddon III
We heard the minx remark	Iolanthe I
We knew your taste	Pirates II
We know him well	Mikado II
We may remark	Princess II
We may succeed--who can foretell?	Yeomen I
We must dance and we must sing	Iolanthe I
We observe too great a stress	Pirates II
We quite understand	Chieftain II
We sail the ocean blue	Pinafore I
We shall all (both) go on requesting	Gondoliers II
We should be, if in Devonshire now	Emerald I
We sounded the trumpet	Cox
We stand, I think	Utopia I
We think we heard him say	Iolanthe I
We triumph now for well we trow	Pirates II
We waste the sunny hours	Beauty I
We were not, thro' some freak of earth	Haddon II
We were shelt'ring	Haddon II
We will dance a cachucha	Gondoliers II
We would be fairly acting	Trial

Wear the flowers	Trial
Wear (Were) this suit	Contrab II
Weep not my friends	Legend 4
Weep ye not for the dead	Light 1
Welcome, gentry, for your entry	Ruddigore I
Welcome, joy! adieu to sadness!	Sorcerer I
Welcome, Sir Knights	Ivanhoe I
Welcome to our hearts again	Iolanthe I
Welcome, welcome with one voice	Exh. Ode
Welcome ye strangers	Beauty I
We'll a memorandum make	Princess II
Well, as I bow'd to his applause	Grand Duke I
We'll charm their senses	Princess I
We'll dance and we'll sing	Contrab II
We'll hear no more	Mikado I
Well may ye ask	Beauty I
We'll shout and sing 'Long live the king'	Princess I
Well, you're a pretty kind of fellow	Grand Duke II
Well, you'r driving like mad	Iolanthe II
Were but I above him	Haddon I
We're called gondolieri	Gondoliers I
Were I a king in very truth	Grand Duke I
Were I thy bride	Yeomen I
We're (Those) pressing prevailers	Gondoliers II
Were you not to Ko-Ko plighted?	Mikado I
West wind blows, The	Haddon II
We've a first-class assortment of magic	Sorcerer I
We've been thrown over	Patience I
What a clever man	Cox
What does it mean?	Rose II
What is the matter	Chieftain II
What these may be, Utopians all	Utopia I
Whatever you are--be that	Utopia II
When a brother leaves his sister	Yeomen II
When a felon's not engaged	Pirates II
When a jester is outwitted	Yeomen II
When a maid is bold and gay	Princess II
When a man has been a naughty baronet	Ruddigore II
When a man's afraid	Mikado II
When a merry maiden marries	Gondoliers I
When a wooer goes a-wooing	Yeomen II

When Alfred's friends (by German)	Emerald I
When all night long a chap remains	Iolanthe II
When anger spreads its wings	Princess II, III
When at my Leonard's deeds sublime	Yeomen I
When Britain really ruled the waves	Iolanthe II
When Britain sounds the trump of war	Utopia I
When but a maid of fifteen year	Utopia II
When darkly looms the day	Iolanthe I
When day is fading	Princess I, III
When first my old, old love I knew	Trial
When Fred'ric was a little lad	Pirates I
When German bands from music stands	Princess III
When he is here I sigh with pleasure	Sorcerer I
When I first put this uniform on	Patience I
When I go out of door	Patience II
When I, good friends	Trial
When I sally forth to seek my prey	Pirates I
When I was a lad I serv'd a term	Pinafore I
When I was but a little lad	Haddon I
When I went to the bar	Iolanthe I
When I'm a bad bart	Ruddigore I
When Islam first arose	Rose I
When it's left to you to say	Utopia I
When jealous torments	Yeomen I
When love and beauty	Sapphire
When maiden loves	Yeomen I
When morning is breaking	Gondoliers I
When my father sent me to Ispahan	Rose I
When off the loser's popp'd	Grand Duke I
When our gallant Norman foes	Yeomen I
When pale afar is the evening star	Haddon I
When she found that he was fickle	Ruddigore II
When the breezes are blowing	Gondoliers I
When the budding bloom of May (spring)	Haddon I
When the buds are blossoming	Ruddigore I
When the enterprising burglar	Pirates II
When the fierce Templar snatched her	Ivanhoe III
When the foeman bares his steel	Pirates II
When the gallant Norman foes	Yeomen I
When the keen axes	Ivanhoe II

When the leaves of autumn sigh	Haddon I
When the nightwind howls	Ruddigore II
When the roseleaf lies on the dew	Beauty I
When thoroughly tired of being admiral	Ruddigore I
When Thou tookest upon Thee	F. Te Deum
When to evade destructions hand	Gondoliers I
When told that they would all be shot	Gondoliers I
When two doughty heroes thunder	Grand Duke I
When two glowing hearts	Grand Duke I
When two heroes once pacific	Grand Duke I
When vespers are ringing	Gondoliers I
When virtuous love is sought	Iolanthe I
When we met at Compostella	Chieftain II
When Wellington thrash'd Bonaparte	Iolanthe II
When yestereve, I knelt to pray	Haddon I
When you find you're a broken-down critter	Grand Duke I
When you had left our pirate fold	Pirates II
When your clothes, from your hat	Grand Duke I
When your lips are all smeary	Grand Duke I
When your mouth is of flannel	Grand Duke II
When you're lying awake	Iolanthe II
Whene'er I poke sarcastic joke	Princess III
Whene'er I spoke	Princess II
Whenever I chance to baffle you	Utopia II
Whenever she condescends to walk	Gondoliers I
Where everyone will rush and run	Rose II
Where the bee sucks there lurk I	Tempest V
Whet the bright steel	Ivanhoe III
Whet the keen axes	Ivanhoe II
Whet ye the steel	Ivanhoe II
While silly servant maidies dress (by German)	Emerald II
While the sun shines	Iolanthe II
While you here do snoring lie	Tempest II
White moon lay	Beauty III
Who am I to raise objection?	Grand Duke I
Who are you, sir?	Cox
Who dares to brag and taunt afar	Kenilworth
Who is it coming under the trees?	Legend 4
Who'd to be robber chief aspire	Contrab II
Who's learnt each vice	Emerald II
Who's not afraid of man or maid	Emerald II

With humbled breast	Iolanthe I
With joy abiding	Princess III
With joyous shout and ringing cheer	Mikado I, II
With laughing song and merry dance	Mikado I, II
With loving and laughing	Gondoliers I
With many a winsome smile	Grand Duke I
With many cheerful facts	Pirates I
With martial gait--with kettle-drums	Rose I
With pas de trois we will conclude	Utopia II
With rage and indignation she is rife	Grand Duke II
With sword and pistol	Contrab I
With sorrow we've nothing to do	Gondoliers I
With Strephon for your foe	Iolanthe I
With wily brain	Utopia II
Within its walls of rock	Yeomen I
Within this breast there beats a heart	Ruddigore I
Wizard thou to guess so well, A	Ivanhoe I
Woe unto them	Prodigal
Woman of the wisest wit, The	Princess II
Women of Adamant	Princess II
Wonderful joy our eyes to bless, A	Utopia II
Won't it be a pretty wedding?	Grand Duke I
Woo thou thy snowflake till she melt	Ivanhoe II
Words of love too loudly spoken	Utopia II
Working monarch, The	Gondoliers II
"Rising early in the morning"	
World is but a broken toy, The	Princess II
World is everything you say, The	Princess II
World where she dwells, The	Emerald I
Would you know the kind of maid	Princess II
Wouldst thou wander	Beauty II
Wreaths of bay and ivy	Grand Duke II

Ye stately homes of England	Haddon I
Ye supple M. P.'s	Ruddigore II
Ye torrents roar	Mikado I
Ye tower warders (yeomen)	Yeomen I
Ye wand'rers from a mighty state	Utopia I

Ye well-to-do squires	Ruddigore II
Yea, though I walk through the valley	Light 2
Yes, I know, that is so	Pinafore II
Yes, Ludwig and his Julia are mated	Grand Duke II
Yes, on reconsideration	Grand Duke II
Yes, she is blithe	Patience I
Yes, yes, in those merry days (The Bouncer's song; "Rataplan")	Cox
Yes, yes, of course you've tried it	Grand Duke I
Yes, yes, we'll subdue it	Princess II
Yet A is happy	Mikado II
Yet his (my) classic lore	Grand Duke II
Yet if the fee is promptly paid	Yeomen I
Yet once again	Antioch 2
Yet the breeze is but a rover	Pirates II
You are, you are! Oh stop, do stop	Miller 3
You booby dense	Grand Duke I
You can spy, sir!	Gondoliers I
You cannot eat breakfast all day	Trial
You do not mean it?	Miller 1
You grow up and you discover	Utopia I
You hold yourself like this	Patience II
You leave us here to watch	On Shore
You may put them on the list	Mikado I
You swindler, you cheat	Cox
You told me you were fair as gold	Pirates I
You understand? Likewise the bride	Ruddigore I
You very, very plain old man	Sorcerer II
You'll lay your head upon your bed	Gondoliers I
You'll say a better major general	Pirates I
Young man, despair	Mikado I
Young Strephon is the kind of lout	Iolanthe I
Your disrespectful sneers	Iolanthe II
Your friendly aid conferred	Utopia I
Your Highness, there's a party	Grand Duke II
Your loyalty our ducal heart-strings touches	Grand Duke II
Your maiden hearts	Patience I
Your powers of observation, O!	Princess II
You're a regular wreck	Iolanthe II
You're very kind	Miller 2
Youth is a boon	Utopia I

Youth will (must), needs have dalliance   Henry 2
   (words by Henry VIII)
   (King Henry's song)

Title, first line, or tune name

ABSENT-MINDED BEGGAR, THE: see When you've shouted "Rule Britannia"	W: Rudyard Kipling
Ah! County Guy, the hour is nigh	W: Sir Walter Scott (from QUENTIN DURWARD)
Aimons-nous, melodie anglaise	
All the dreaming is broken through	W: Harrison Millard
All this night bright angels sing	T: arr. of old carol H W: William Austin
And God shall wipe away all tears (from THE LIGHT OF THE WORLD, see also Index I)	
Angel Gabriel	
Angel voices: see Stars of the evening, softly gleaming	
Another sun shines bright!	
ANSWER, THE: see THE WINDOW, no. 9	
ARABIAN LOVE SONG: see My faint spirit was sitting	
ARIEL'S SONG: see Come unto these yellow sands (from THE TEMPEST, see Index I)	
Art thou weary, art thou languid	T: Rest (Venite) H W: tr. by J. M. Neale
Aspiration, or Propior Dio: see Nearer my God, to Thee	
AT THE WINDOW: see THE WINDOW, no. 2	
At Thine altar, Lord, we gather	T: Dulce sonans H W: Mary Bradford Whiting
Aube nait et ta porte est close, L' (Morning dawns): see OH! MY CHARMER	
Audite audientes me: see I heard the voice of Jesus say	
AY: see THE WINDOW, no. 10	
AY DE MI, MY BIRD: see THE YOUNG MOTHER, no. 2	

Be merry, all birds, to-day: see THE
   WINDOW, no. 10
Be Thou with us every day   T: Litany no. 3   H
                               W: T. B. Pollock

Beautiful, sublime, and glorious   W: Bernard Barton   PS
BELEAGURED, THE: see Fling wide the
   gates!
Bethlehem: see While shepherds watched
   their flocks
BID ME AT LEAST GOOD-BYE: see 'Tis
   twenty years since our last meeting
Birds in the night that softly call   T: from Cox and Box
                                   "Hush'd is the bacon"
                                 W: Lionel H. Lewin

Birds' love and birds' song; see THE
   WINDOW, no. 5
Birds their hymn have caroll'd
Bishopgarth: see O God, the Ruler of our
   race; O King of Kings; Lord of Hosts
   our King shall be, The
Bolwell: see Thou to whom the sick and
   dying; Lord of might, our land's
   defender (a coronation hymn)
BRIDE FROM THE NORTH: see The shadows
   take their flight
Bright o'er the lagoon (from THE MER-   W: F. Rizzelli
   CHANT OF VENICE)   Eng. by Will Ransom
Brightly gleams our banner   T: St. Theresa   H
                                 W: T. J. Potter

Britain fought her sons: see EXHIBI-
   TION ODE
Britons, hold your own! see EXHIBI-
   TION ODE

Calm be our rest tonight   W: Robert Steele
Calm was the hallowed night   W: Charlotte Elliott   PS
CARE IS ALL FIDDLE-DE-DEE (from THE
   MILLER AND HIS MAN, see Index I)

CAROL FOR CHRISTMAS DAY: see All
   this night bright angels sing

Carrow: see My God, I thank Thee

Chapel Royal: see O love that wilt not let
   me go

Children, send a song of praise (TWO   W: C. H. Lloyd   H
   HYMNS FOR CHILDREN)

CHORISTER, THE: see O sweet and dim
   the light and shade; THE YOUNG
   MOTHER, no. 3

Christ is risen!   T: Resurrexit   H
                                   W: A. T. Gurney

CHRISTMAS BELLS AT SEA: see Still
   the night and calm the ocean

Christus: see Show me not only Jesus
   dying

THE CHURCH HAS WAITED LONG: see
   O where shall rest be found

Clarence: see Winter reigneth o'er the
   land

Coena Domini: see Draw nigh, and take
   the body of the Lord

Come, Holy Ghost, our souls inspire   T: Veni, Creator   H
                                 W: tr. by Bishop
                                     John Cosin

Come to me, O ye children   W: H. W. Long-
                                 fellow

Come, ye faithful, raise the strain   T: St. Kevin   H
                               W: tr. by John
                               Mason Neale

COMING HOME: see While swiftly the
   tide

Constance: see Who trusts in God

Coronae: see Crown Him with many
   crowns

CORONATION HYMN: see Lord of
   Might

Could ye come back to me

COUNTY GUY: see Ah! County Guy, the
   hour is nigh

Courage brother! do not stumble   W: Norman Macleod H

CRADLE SONG, OR LITTLE DARLING,
  SLEEP AGAIN: see THE YOUNG
  MOTHER, no. 1

Crown Him with many crowns   T: Coronae   H
  W: Matthew Bridges

Cum sancto spiritu, fugue   W: Liturgical Chorus &
  Orchestra

Daughters of Jerusalem weep not (from
  THE LIGHT OF THE WORLD, see
  Index I)

Day, a week, a month, are past, A   W: Samuel K.
  Cowan

Day is cold and dark and dreary, The   W: H. W. Long-   PS
  (no. 1 of SIX FOUR-PART SONGS)   fellow

Deep on the convent roof   W: Alfred, Lord   PS
  Tennyson

DISTANT SHORE, THE: see A maiden
  sat at her door

Domine salvam fac Reginam: see TE
  DEUM

DOMINION HYMN: see God bless our
  wide dominion

DOVE SONG: see When sleep descends
  on mortals

Draw nigh, and take the body of the Lord   T: Coena Domini   H
  W: tr. by J. M.
  Neale

Dulce sonans, or Dulci sonantia: see At
  Thine altar, Lord, we gather

E tu nol sai (You sleep) (serenata in   W: Italian by G.
  A. W. Pinero's THE PROFLIGATE)   Mazzacato
  English by B. C.
  Stephenson

Ecclesia: see O where shall rest be found
ECHOES: see How sweet the answer
EDWARD GRAY: see Sweet Emma More-
   land
Evelyn: see In the hour of my distress
EVENING: see Peace breathes along the
   shades
EVENING HYMN: see O gladsome light
   (from THE GOLDEN LEGEND, see
   Index I)
EVER: see In waves the music rose and
   fell!
Ever faithful, ever sure: see Let us with
   a gladsome mind

EXHIBITION ODE: W: Alfred, Lord
   (Written for the opening of the Colonial   Tennyson
   and Indian Exhibition, 1886)   Chorus &
     1. Welcome, welcome with on voice   Orchestra
     2. May we find, as ages run
     3. Britain fought her sons of yore
     4. Britons, hold your own!
     5. Sharers of our glorious past

Fair daffodils, we weep to see   W: Robert Herrick   PS
Falfield, or Formosa: see Love Divine,
   all love excelling
Father of Heaven, Who hast created all   T: St. Francis   H
                                   W: tr. by Catherine
                                      Winkworth

Father, Thy children bow in adoration   W: adapted by   PS
                                   A. F. Andrews

Fatherland, or St. Edmund: see We are
   but strangers here
Fear not, ye seek Jesus (from THE LIGHT   arr. by Geo.   PS
   OF THE WORLD   B. Nevin
FESTIVAL TE DEUM: see TE DEUM
Few more years shall roll, A   T: Leominster; arr.   H
                                     from G. W. Martin
                                   W: Horatius Bonar

FIRST DEPARTURE, THE: see THE
    YOUNG MOTHER, no. 3

FIVE SHAKESPEARE SONGS:
1. O mistress mine (from TWELFTH
   NIGHT)
2. Orpheus with his lute (from
   HENRY VIII)
3. ROSALIND: <u>first line:</u>
       From the east to western Ind
       (from AS YOU LIKE IT)
4. Sigh no more, ladies (from MUCH
   ADO ABOUT NOTHING)
5. THE WILLOW SONG: <u>first line:</u>
       A poor soul sat sighing (from
       OTHELLO)

Fling wide the gates!
    W: Henry F. Chorley   PS

For all Thy love and goodness
    T: Springtime; arr. from Aldrich   H
    W: Frances J. Douglas & Bishop W. Walsham How

For ever with the Lord
    T: Nearer home; arr. from J. Woodbury   H
    W: James Montgomery

FOR LOVE ALONE: see Love feeds on
    many kinds of food (from THE
    SORCERER, see Index I)

<u>Formosa</u>, or <u>Falfield:</u> see Love Divine
    all love excelling; Praise the Lord!
    ye heavens, adore him; Glorious things
    of Thee are spoken

<u>Fortunatus:</u> see Welcome, happy morning

From Egypt's bondage come
    T: Pilgrimage   H
    W: T. Kelly

Frost is here, The: see THE WINDOW,
    no. 4

Fugue 'Cum sancto spiritu'
    W: Liturgical Chorus & Orchestra

Gennesareth, or Heber, or Succour: see
    When through the torn sail
Gentle shepherd, or The long home: see
    Tender shepherd
GIVE: see See the rivers flowing
Glorious company of the apostles, The:
    see TE DEUM
Glorious things of Thee are spoken   T: Formosa (Fal-
                                    field)

Glowing with love, on fire for fame   W: Sir Walter
                                      Scott

God bless our wide dominion (Dominion   W: adapted from a
    hymn)   poem of Marquis
                                      de Lorne (John
                                      George E. H.
                                      Douglas S. Camp-
                                      bell, 9th Duke of
                                      Argyll)

God moves in a mysterious way   T: St. Nathaniel   H
                                    W: Wm. Cowper

God of my life *(arr. H. R. Shelley)
GOD SHALL WIPE AWAY ALL TEARS
    (from THE LIGHT OF THE WORLD,
    see Index I)
God the All-Terrible!   T: Ultor omnipotens   H
                                    W: Henry F. Chorley
                                      & John Ellerton

God the Father   T: Litany no. 3
GOLDEN DAYS: see Once in the days of
    golden weather
Golden Sheaves: see To Thee, O Lord, our
    hearts we raise
Gone! gone, till the end of the year: see
    THE WINDOW, no. 3
Good old year's a waning, The   W: Henry F. Chorley
Great Father, when my eyes behold
Great King of nations, hear our prayer   T: Old 137th Psalm;   H
                                      arr. from Genevan
                                      Psalter
                                      W: J. Hampden
                                      Gurney

*Only in Pazdirek

GUINEVERE: see There was deep calm
shade

Hail glorious song!	W: Clifton O. PS Page arr. by Chas. T. Mac- Lary

Hanford: see Jesus, my Saviour, look on me
Happy children we have been (from TWO
   HYMNS FOR CHILDREN)   H

Hark! a thrilling voice is sounding   T: Lux eoi   H
                                 W: tr. by Edw.
                                 Caswall

Hark! what mean those holy voices?   PS
   (Christmas Carol)
He is coming   T: Formosa (Fal- H
                                 field)

He is gone--a cloud of light   T: St. Patrick H
                                 W: A. P. Stanley

He will return (from CONTRABANDISTA,
   see Index I)
Heal me, O my Saviour   W: Godfrey Thring H
Hearken unto me my people   W: from ISAIAH   PS
                                 51:4-6

HEAVEN IS MY HOME: see I am but a
   stranger here
Heber, or Gennesereth, or Succour: see
   When through the torn sail
HIGHLAND MESSAGE, THE: see Thou'rt
   passing hence
His temple is not made with hands
Holy City: see Sing alleluia forth in
   duteous praise
Holy Spirit! come in might!   T: Light; arr. from H
                                 S. Webbe's collec-
                                 tion
                                 W: tr. by Edw.
                                 Caswall

Homeland! the homeland! the land of the freeborn	W: Rev. H. R. Haweis (solo version arr. by J. E. Newell)	PS
How sweet the answer (no. 6 of SIX FOUR-PART SONGS)	W: Thomas Moore	PS
Hush! I cannot bear to see thee	W: Adelaide A Proctor	
Hush thee, my babie (perhaps identical with "O, hush thee my babie")		
Hushed was the evening hymn	W: James D. Burns	H
HYMN OF THE HOMELAND, A: see The Homeland		

I am but a stranger here	W: T. R. Taylor	
"I can scarcely hear" she murmur'd	W: Adelaide A. Proctor	
I had a dream tonight	W: Rev. Wm. Barnes	
I hear the soft note of my Saviour's voice	W: J. E. Middleton	
I heard a voice long years ago (Qu'elle etait douce)	W: Fr. words by D. Tagliafico; Eng. by Louisa Gray	
I heard the nightingale	W: Rev. C. H. Townshend	
I heard the voice of Jesus say	T: Audite audientes me W: Horatius Bonar	H
I linger round the very spot	W: Lionel H. Lewin	
I met my love in a dream last night	W: J. P. Douglas	
I need Thee precious Jesus	W: F. Whitfield	
I shaded mine eyes one day	W: Jean Ingelow	
I sing the birth (Christmas carol)	W: Ben Jonson	PS
I will lay me down in peace	W: Psalm 4:9	PS
I will mention the loving-kindnesses	W: Psalm 63	PS
I will sing of Thy power	W: Psalm 59	PS
I will worship towards Thy holy temple		PS

I wish to tune my quiv'ring lyre
W: Ode from Ana-
creon tr. by Lord
Byron

I would I were a king ("Enfant, si j'etais roi")
W: Victor Hugo
tr. by Sir Alexander
Cockburn

If doughty deeds my lady please
W: Graham of Gart-
mor

If I were a king (perhaps the same as "I would I were a king")

If ye be risen with Christ (from THE LIGHT OF THE WORLD, see Index I)

IMPERIAL INSTITUTE ODE:
W: Lewis Morris   Chorus
& Orchestra

   (Ode written and composed expressly for the occasion of laying the foundation stone of the Imperial Institute by Her Majesty the Queen in 1887)
1. With voice and solemn music
2. Close on their steps
3. No more we seek our realms increase
4. First lady of our English race
5. Oh, may the hand which rules our fate

In his mother's pure embrace
W: W. J. C.

In memoriam: see Lord, keep us safe this night

In the hour of my distress
T: Evelyn   H
W: Robert Herrick

IN THE SUMMER'S LONG AGO, or MY LOVE BEYOND THE SEA: see I met my love in a dream last night

In the twilight of our love
T: from PATIENCE,
"Silver'd is the
raven hair"
W: Hugh Conway

In war's stern panoply
W: J. P. Douglas

In waves the music rose and fell!
W: Mrs. Bloomfield
Moore

INVOCATION TO SONG: see Hail glorious song!

It came upon the midnight clear	T: Noel; arr. of traditional air	H
	W: E. H. Sears	
IT IS NOT LOVE: see Thou hast the pow'r (from THE SORCERER, see Index I)		
It was a lover and his lass	W: Wm. Shakespeare Duet, with Chorus	
IT'S O MY LOVE, MY LOVE: see The snow lies white		
Jesu, in Thy dying woes	W: Litany no. 3; arr. of traditional melody	H
Jesu, life of those who die	T: Litany no. 2	H
	W: T. B. Pollock	
Jesu, my Saviour, look on me	T: Hanford	H
	W: Charlotte Elliott	
Jesu, we are far away	T: Litany no. 1	H
	W: T. B. Pollock	
Joy to the victors (no. 4 of SIX FOUR-PART SONGS)	W: Sir Walter Scott	PS
JUBILATE DEO in D major: see O be joyful in the Lord; TE DEUM, JUBILATE AND KYRIE IN D		
KING HENRY'S SONG: "Youth will needs have dalliance" (from HENRY VIII, see Index I)		
KYRIE IN D MAJOR: see TE DEUM, JUBILATE and KYRIE IN D		

Lacrymae: see Lord, in this, Thy mercy's
   day
LAST NIGHT OF THE YEAR, THE: see
   The good old year's a waning
Lead, kindly light   T: Lux in tenebrae   PS
                                            W: John H. Newman

Lebbaeus (same tune as Litany no. 3)
Leominster: see A few more years shall
   roll
LET ME DREAM AGAIN: see The sun is
   setting (Composed expressly for Madame
   Christine Nilsson)
Let no tears to-day be shed   T: St. Millinent   H
                                            W: tr. by R. F.
                                               Littledale

Let others seek the peaceful plain (from
   CONTRABANDISTA, see Index I)
Let our choir new anthems raise   W. J. M. Neale
Let us with a gladsome mind   T: Ever faithful,   H
                                               ever sure
                                            W: John Milton

LETTER, THE: see THE WINDOW, no. 6
LIFE THAT LIVES FOR YOU, A: see The
   sweet seductive arts
Light: see Holy Spirit! come in might!
Light, so low upon earth: see THE
   WINDOW, no. 12
Lights and shadows fly, The: see THE
   WINDOW, no. 1
Lights on yonder snowy range, The   W: Aubrey de   PS
   (no. 5 of SIX FOUR-PART SONGS)   Vere
Litany no. 1: see Jesu, we are far away
Litany no. 2: see Jesu, life of those who
   die
Litany no. 3: see Jesu, in Thy dying woes;
   Be Thou with us every day; God the
   Father
LITTLE DARLING, SLEEP AGAIN: see THE
   YOUNG MOTHER, no. 1
Little feet are passing
Little maid of Arcadee (from THESPIS,
   see Index I)

LIVING POEMS: see Come to me, O ye
  children
LONG DAY CLOSES, THE: see No star is
  o'er the lake; Saviour, Thy children
  keep
Long home, The or Gentle shepherd: see
  Tender shepherd
LONGING FOR HOME: see I shaded mine
  eyes one day
LOOKING BACK (UNE VOIX DU PASSE):
  see I heard a voice long years ago
LOOKING FORWARD: see Only a tress of
  hair

Lord, in this, Thy mercy's day
T: Lacrymae   H
W: Isaac Williams

LORD IS RISEN, THE: see Fear not, ye
  seek Jesus (from THE LIGHT OF THE
  WORLD, see Index I)

Lord, keep us safe this night (vesper hymn)
T: adapted from his
  "IN MEMORIAM"
W: George Roberts (?)

Lord of Hosts our King shall be, The
T: Bishopgarth
W: Rev. C. A.
  Alington

Lord of Might, our land's Defender
  (CORONATION HYMN)
T: Bolwell   H
W: Mary Bradford
  Whiting

LOST CHORD, THE (DER VERKLUNGENE
  TON; L'ACCORD PERDU): see Seated
  one day at the organ
Love Divine, all love excelling
T: Fairfield   H
  (Formosa)
W: Charles Wesley

Love laid his sleepless head (Interpolated
  in the Gaiety Theatre production of THE
  MERRY WIVES OF WINDSOR, see also
  Index I)
W: Algernon C.
  Swinburne

LOVE THAT LOVES ME NOT, THE: see
  When the cold shadows gloam
LOVER'S DUET (LOVE DUET (?) from THE
  PIRATES OF PENZANCE II (?)
LULLABY, A: see Birds in the night

75

Lux eoi: see Hark! a thrilling voice is
   sounding
Lux mundi: see O Jesu, Thou art standing
Lux in tenebrae: see Lead, kindly light

MAIDEN'S STORY, THE: see The maiden
   sat at her busy wheel
Maiden sat at her busy wheel, The   W: Emma Embury
Maiden sat at her door, A   W: W. S. Gilbert
Marlborough: see O strength and stay up-
   holding all creation
Marquis de Mincepie (from THE MILLER
   AND HIS MAN, see Index I)
MARRIAGE MORNING: see THE WINDOW,
   no. 12
MARY MORISON: see O Mary, at thy
   window
May we find, as ages run: see EXHIBI-
   TION ODE
Mercy and truth are met together (adapted   PS
   and arr. from Russian church music)
Merry Christmas to you all (from THE
   MILLER AND HIS MAN, see Index I)
METHOUGHT THE STARS WERE BLINKING   W: Jean Ingelow
   BRIGHT: see O fair dove
Mist and the rain, The: see THE WINDOW,
   no. 7
Moon in silent brightness, The   W: Bishop Reginald
                                              Heber
Moon no longer rules on high, The   W: English words by
   (serenata in A. W. Pinero's THE   B. C. Stephenson
   PROFLIGATE)   Italian by G.
                                              Mazzacato
Morn, happy morn (in the play OLIVIA   TRIO
   by W. G. Wills)
Morning dawns and thou still art hidden:
   see OH! MY CHARMER

MOTHER'S DREAM, THE: see I'd a dream
   tonight
Mount Zion: see Rock of Ages, cleft for me
MY CHILD AND I: see Once I used to dream

My dear and only love   W: The Marquis
                                        of Montrose
                                        (A.D. 1640)

MY DEAREST HEART: see All the dream-
   ing
My faint spirit was sitting   W: Percy B.
                                        Shelley

My God, I thank Thee   T: Carrow   H
                                        W: Adelaide A.
                                        Proctor

My heart is like a silent lute   W: Benjamin
                                        Disraeli (from
                                        HENRIETTA
                                        TEMPLE)

MY LOVE: see There sits a bird
MY LOVE BEYOND THE SEA, or IN THE
   SUMMER'S LONG AGO: see I met my
   love in a dream last night
MY LOVE WE'LL MEET AGAIN (from
   CONTRABANDISTA; see Index I)
MY TIMES ARE IN THY HANDS: see To
   mourn our dead

Nearer home: see For ever with the Lord
Nearer, my God, to Thee   T: Propior Deo or   H
                                          Aspiration
                                        W: Sarah F. Adams

Nel ciel seren, di stelle (from THE
   MERCHANT OF VENICE; see Index I)
Night is calm and cloudless, The (from
   THE GOLDEN LEGEND; see Index I)
NIGHT WIND SIGHS ALONE: see The
   tinkling sheepbell knells
NO ANSWER: see THE WINDOW, no. 7,
   no. 8

No star is o'er the lake   W: Henry F.   PS
                                              Chorley

Noel: see It came upon the midnight
   clear
NONE BUT I CAN SAY: see The noonday
   sun was fierce and bright
Noonday sun was fierce and bright, The   W: Lionel H. Lewin

O be joyful in the Lord (JUBILATE DEO
   IN D MAJOR): see TE DEUM
O bird that used to press (AY DE MI, MY
   BIRD): see THE YOUNG MOTHER, no.
   2
O diviner air   W: Alfred, Lord   Duet
                                              Tennyson
O fair dove! O fond dove!   W: Jean Ingelow
O foolish fay (from IOLANTHE; see Index I)
O gladsome light (from THE GOLDEN   PS
   LEGEND; see Index I)
O God, our help in ages past: see TE   T: adapted from   PS
   DEUM, 1872   Sullivan's arr. of
                                          St. Ann by Sir
                                        Frederick Bridges
                                W: Isaac Watts
O God, the Ruler of our race   T: Bishopgarth   H
                                W: Mary Bradford
                                          Whiting
O God, Thour art worthy to be praised   PS
O hearken Thou unto the voice of my   arr. and adapted by
   calling   Sir Frederick Bridge PS
                                W: Psalm V:2
O hush thee, my babie (no. 2 of SIX
   FOUR-PART SONGS)   W: Sir Walter   PS
                                    Scott
O Israel! return, return to the Lord   W: from HOSEA
                                  14:1, 2
O Jesu, our salvation   T: Lux mundi   H
                              W: James Hamilton

O Jesu, Thou art standing	T: Lux mundi H W: Bp. W. Walsham How
O King of Kings (QUEEN'S JUBILEE HYMN): ("To be sung in all churches Sunday, June 20, 1897"; written for Queen Victoria's Diamond Jubilee, the sixtieth year of her reign, 1897)	T: Bishopgarth H W: Bp. W. Walsham How
O Lord, let Thy mercy: see TE DEUM	
O Lord, on this last holy day	
O Lord, save Thy people: see TE DEUM	
O love that wilt not let me go	T: Chapel Royal H W: George Matheson
O love the Lord, all ye his saints	W: Psalm 31:26-27 PS
O Mary, at thy window	W: Robert Burns
O mistress mine (see FIVE SHAKESPEARE SONGS)	
O moon, art thou clad (from IVANHOE; see Index I)	
O paradise! O paradise!	T: Paradise H W: F. W. Faber
O strength and stay upholding all creation	T: Marlborough; H arr. of old tune W: tr. by John Ellerton
O swallow, swallow flying, flying South	W: Alfred, Lord Tennyson (from THE PRINCESS)
O sweet and dim, the light and shade (THE CHORISTER; see THE YOUNG MOTHER, no. 3)	W: F. E. Weatherly
O taste and see how gracious the Lord is	PS
O! TELL ME HOW TO WOO THEE: see If doughty deeds	
O tell me, pretty river!	
O! that thou had'st hearkened (from THE PRODIGAL SON; see Index I)	arr. by Homer N. PS Bartlett
O thou before whom open lies	T: Jubilee tune of Sullivan W: Rev. S. C. Lowry

O where shall rest be found	T: Ecclesia H
	W: James Montgomery
ODE: see EXHIBITION ODE; IMPERIAL INSTITUTE ODE	
Of Thy love some gracious token	T: Of Thy love, or H
	St. Lucien
	W: T. Kelly
Oh bella mia (Italian version of SWEET DREAMER): see OH! MY CHARMER	
OH! MA CHARMANTE (French version of SWEET DREAMER) see OH! MY CHARMER	
OH! MY CHARMER, or SWEET DREAMER	W: Victor Hugo
L'aube nait et ta porte est close	tr. or adapted
Oh! bella mia	by H. B. Farnie
Tho' heaven's gate of light uncloses	by H. B. Farnie
Morning dawns and thou still are hidden	?
Oh sweet and fair	W: A.F.C.K.
Oh, take this flow'r, dear love!	W: W. S. Gilbert
OLD LOVE LETTERS: see A day, a week, a month	
Old 137th Psalm: see Great King of Nations, hear our prayer	
On, Christmas night, full round and bright	
ON THE HILL: see The lights and shadows fly	
ONCE AGAIN: see I linger round the very spot	
Once I used to dream	W: F. E. Weatherly
Once in the days of golden weather	W: Lionel H. Lewin
Only a tress of hair	W: Louisa Gray
ONLY THE NIGHT WIND SIGHS ALONE: see The Tinkling sheepbells	
Onward, Christian soldiers	T: St. Gertrude H
	W: Sabine Baring-Gould
Orpheus with his lute: see FIVE SHAKESPEARE SONGS	
OTHER DAYS: see When we were young	
Our Blest Redeemer, ere He breathed	T: Promissio Patris H
	W: Harriet Auber

Our boys across the sea
Over the roof (from THE SAPPHIRE
    NECKLACE; see Index I)

Palmy isles, like jewels strew
Paradise: see O Paradise
Parting: see With the sweet word of
    peace
PARTING GLEAMS: see The lights on
    yonder snowy range
Peace breathes along the shades (no. 3 of   W: J. W. Goethe   PS
    SIX FOUR-PART SONGS)   tr. by Lord
                                    Houghton

Pilgrimage: see From Egypt's bondage come
Poor soul sat sighing, A: see FIVE SHAKE-
    SPEARE SONGS
Praise the Lord! ye heavens, adore him   T: Formosa   H
                                W: Bishop Richard
                                  Mant

Propior Dio, or Aspiration: see Nearer,
    my God, to Thee
Promissio Patris: see Our blest Redeemer
PSALM (in German)   Chorus &
                                    Orchestra

Psalm: Old 137th: see Great King of Na-
    tions, hear our prayer

QUEEN'S JUBILEE HYMN: see O King of
    Kings
Qu'elle etait douce et que de fois: see I
    heard a voice long years ago

RAINY DAY, THE: see The day is cold and
    dark and dreary
Refrain thy voice from weeping
Rejoice in the Lord   W: Rev. R. Brown-   PS
                                               Borthwick

Rest: see Art thou weary, art thou languid
Resurrexit: see Christ is risen!
Rhagom, filwyr Jesu (Welsh text for "On-
    ward, Christian soldiers")
RIVER, THE: see O tell me, pretty river
Rock of ages, cleft for me   T: Mount Zion   H
                                              W: A. M. Toplady

ROSALIND: see FIVE SHAKESPEARE
    SONGS
Roseate hues of early dawn, The   W: Cecil F.   PS
                                             Alexander

SAD MEMORIES: see The wind now is
    weary
Safe home, safe home in port   W: tr. by J. M.   H
                                           Neale

SAILOR'S GRAVE, THE: see There is in
    the wide lone sea
ST. AGNES' EVE: see Deep on the convent
    roof
St. Ann: see The Son of God goes forth to
    war
St. Edmund, or Fatherland: see We are   H
    but strangers here
St. Francis: see Father of Heaven, who
    hast created all
St. Gertrude: see Onward, Christian
    soldiers
St. Kevin: see Come, ye faithful, raise
    the strain
St. Lucian: see Of Thy love some gracious
    token
St. Luke, or St. Nathaniel: see God moves
    in a mysterious way

St. Mary Magdalene: see Saviour, when
   in dust to Thee

St. Millicent: see Let no tears today be
   shed

St. Nathaniel, or St. Luke: see God moves
   in a mysterious way

St. Patrick: see He is gone--a cloud of
   light

St. Theresa: see Brightly gleams our
   banner

Saints of God, their conflict past, The
                                    T: Saints of God   H
                                      W: Arachbishop W.D.
                                            Maclagan

Samuel (same tune as Hushed was the
   evening hymn)

Saviour, Thy children keep
                                    T: The long day   PS
                                        closes
                                    W: adapted by
                                        Robert Steele

Saviour, when in dust to Thee
                                    T: St. Mary   H
                                      Magdalene
                                    W: Robert Grant

Say, watchman, what of the night?
   (identical with (?) Watchman,
   what of the night)
                                                               PS

SEASIDE THOUGHTS: see Beautiful,
   sublime, and glorious

Seated one day at the organ
                                    W: Adelaide A.
                                      Proctor

See the rivers flowing
                                    W: Adelaide A.
                                      Proctor

SERVICE: see TE DEUM, JUBILATE,
   KYRIE IN D MAJOR (1866)

Service due to God, The

SHADOW, A: see What lack the valleys

Shadows of the evening blessing

Shadows of the evening hours

Shadows take their flight, The
                                    W: Henry F. Chorley

SHAKESPEARE SONGS: see FIVE SHAKE-
   SPEARE SONGS

She is not fair to outward view
                                    W: Hartley Coleridge

Show me not only Jesus dying	T: Christus H W: Josiah Condor
Sigh no more, ladies: see FIVE SHAKE- SPEARE SONGS	
Sing alleluia forth in duteous praise	T: Holy City H W: tr. by John Ellerton
Sing, O heavens	W: from ISIAH: PS 49, 25; PSALMS 85, 45
Sing unto the Lord and praise His name	PS
SISTERS, THE: see O diviner air	
Sleep, my love, sleep	W: G. J. Whyte- Melville
Snow lies white, The	W: Jean Ingelow
Sometimes, when I'm sitting alone	W: Lady Lindsay (of Balcarres)
Son of God goes forth to war, The	T: St. Ann, arr. PS from Wm. Croft W: Bishop Reginald Heber
SONG OF PEACE (from ON SHORE AND SEA, see Index I)	
SONG OF THE HOMELAND, A: see The Homeland	
SONG OF THE WRENS, THE or THE WINDOW: see THE WINDOW, no. 6; Where is another sweet	
SPRING: see THE WINDOW, no. 5	
Springtime: see For all Thy love and goodness	
Stars of evening, softly gleaming	T: Angel voices H W: Mary Bradford Whiting
Still the night and calm the ocean	W: Chas. L. Kenney
Strain upraise of joy and praise, The	W: J. M. Neale PS
Succour: see When through the torn sail	
Sun comes, moon comes: see THE WINDOW, no. 11	
Sun is setting, The	W: B. C. Stephenson

Sweet day, so cool (dedicated to Jenny-Lind-Goldschmidt)	W:	George Herbert
SWEET DREAMER: see OH! MY CHARMER		
Sweet Emma Moreland	W:	Alfred, Lord Tennyson
Sweet Saviour! bless us ere we go	T:	Valete
	W:	F. W. Faber
Sweet seductive arts, The	W:	Lionel H. Lewin
SWEETHEARTS: see Oh, take this flow'r, dear love		

TE DEUM, JUBILATE AND KYRIE IN D*	W:	Liturgical PS
TE DEUM LAUDAMUS and DOMINE SALVAM FAC REGINAM... (for the festival of May 1, 1872 in celebration of the recovery of H. R. H. the Prince of Wales, after wards Edward VII**	W:	Liturgical Chorus & Orchestra
TE DEUM LAUDAMUS. A thanksgiving for victory. 1900*** Contents of the TE DEUM (1872, 1900): Glorious company of the apostles, The O Lord, let Thy mercy O Lord, save Thy people To Thee Cherubin Vouchsafe, O Lord We believe that Thou shalt come We praise Thee, O God When Thou tookest upon Thee	W:	Liturgical Chorus & Orchestra

* Also referred to as the SERVICE (1866, 1872)
** Generally known as the Festival Te Deum.
*** Posthumous publication. Performed in 1902 at the close of the South African War.

(Festival) TE DEUM. *

Tears, idle tears, I know not what they mean — W: Alfred, Lord Tennyson (from THE PRINCESS)

TELL ME HOW TO WOO THEE: see If doughty deeds

TENDER AND TRUE: see Could ye come back to me

Tender Shepherd, Thou has still'd — T: Gentle shepherd or The long home — H
W: J. W. Meinhold tr. by Catherine Winkworth

TENNYSON SONGS: see THE WINDOW, or THE SONG OF THE WRENS

There is in the wide lone sea — W: H. F. Lyte

There is joy in the presence

There is none like unto the God of Jeshurun (completion of an anthem by John Goss) — PS

There sits a bird on yonder tree — W: Richard H. Barham (from THE INGOLDSBY LEGENDS)

There was deep calm shade — W: Lionel H. Lewin

They laid Him in the tomb

THOU ART LOST TO ME: see Tho' we're parted by land and sea

Thou'rt passing hence, my brother — W: Felicia D. (Browne) Hemans

THOU ART WEARY: see Hush! I cannot bear to see thee

Thou God of Love, beneath Thy sheltering wings — W: Jane Euphemia Browne — H

* GROVE'S DICTIONARY OF MUSIC AND MUSICIANS, (1955) v. 8, p. 183: "Festival Te Deum. Liturgical. Chester Festival, 1897." It is not clear which TE DEUM this refers to. Same reference appears in Oscar Thompson's THE INTERNATIONAL CYCLOPEDIA OF MUSIC AND MUSICIANS, 7th ed. 1956, p. 1830.

Thou hast the pow'r (from SORCERER, see
    Index I)

Thou, oh Lord, art our Father

Thou, to Whom the sick and dying   T: Bolwell   H
                                        W: Godfrey Thring

Thou wast that all to me, love   W: Edgar Allan Poe

Tho' heaven's gate of light uncloses: see
    OH! MY CHARMER

Tho' we're parted by land and sea

Through sorrow's path   W: H. Kirke White   PS

Tinkling sheepbell knells the parting day
    (from CONTRABANDISTA, see Index I)

'Tis the midwatch of night

'Tis twenty years since our last meeting
    (in Sydney Grundy's AN OLD JEW)

To mourn our dead we gather here   T: Victoria   H
                                          W: Mary Bradford
                                                 Whiting

TO ONE IN PARADISE: see Thou wast
    that all to me, love

To Thee Cherubin: see TE DEUM

To Thee, O Lord, our hearts we raise   T: Golden sheaves   H
                                          W: W. Chatterton Dix

TROUBADOUR, THE: see Glowing with
    love, on fire for fame

Tui sunt coeli

Turn Thee again, O Lord (adapted and arr.   PS
    from Russian church music)

Turn Thy face from my sins   W: Psalm 51:9,10,   PS
                                        11

TWELVE TENNYSON SONGS: see THE
    WINDOW

TWO HYMNS FOR CHILDREN   H

Two little hands that meet: see THE WIN-
    DOW, no. 9

Ultor omnipotens: see God the All-Terrible
Upon the snow-clad earth (Christmas carol)   PS

Valete: see Sweet Saviour! bless us ere
 we go
VENETIAN SERENADE: see Nel ciel seren;
 Bright o'er the lagoon
Veni, Creator: see Come, Holy Ghost, our
 souls inspire
Venite, or Rest: see Art thou weary, art thou
 languid
VERKLUNGENE TON, DER (THE LOST CHORD):
 see Seated one day at the organ
VESPER HYMN: see Lord, keep us safe this
 night
Victoria: see To mourn our dead we gather
 here
Village chimes, those dear old chimes, The   W: Chas. J. Rowe
Vine, vine and eglantine; see THE WINDOW,
 no. 2
Vouchsafe, O Lord: see TE DEUM

Wake, gentle maiden (from CONTRABANDISTA,
 see Index I)
WATCHMAN, WHAT OF THE NIGHT?   PS
 (identical with(?) "Say, watchman, what
 of the night?")
Way is long and dreary, The   W: Adelaide A.   PS
                                                      Proctor
We are but strangers here (funeral hymn)   T: Fatherland, or   H
                                                      St. Edmund
                                                  W: T. R. Taylor
                                                      (or Jackson (?)
We believe that Thou shalt come: see TE
 DEUM

We have heard with our ears, O God	W: Psalm 44 PS
We've ploughed our land	
We praise Thee, O God: see TE DEUM	
Weary lot is thine, fair maid, A	W: Sir Walter Scott
Welcome, happy morning!	T: Welcome, happy H
	morning, or Fortuna-
	tus
	W: tr. by John Ellerton
Welcome, welcome with one voice: see EXHIBITION ODE	
West is red with sunset's glow, The	
What does little birdie say?	W: Alfred, Lord
	Tennyson (from
	SEA DREAMS)
What lack the valleys	W: Adelaide A.
	Proctor
WHEN: see THE WINDOW, no. 11	
When dark grey clouds come rolling fast	
When love and beauty to be married go	PS
(from THE SAPPHIRE NECKLACE, see Index I)	
When my evening pray'r is spoken*	W: H. F. Chorley
When sleep descends on mortals	
When the cold shadows gloam	W: W. S. Gilbert
When thou art away, love	W: W. J. Stewart
WHEN THOU ART NEAR: see When thou art away, love	
When Thou tookest upon thee: see TE DEUM	
When through the torn sail	T: Heber, or H
	Gennesareth, or
	Succour
	W: Reginald Heber
When we were young	W: Harry Graham, from
	the French of C. F.
	Panard (1674-1765)
When you've shouted "Rule Britannia"	W: Rudyard Kipling

* This is followed by: "Our Father Who
  in Heaven dost dwell" but there is no
  music with it, in HYMNS FOR
  CHILDREN.

Where is another sweet as my sweet?: see
 THE WINDOW, no. 6

While shepherds watched their flocks by
 night

T: Bethlehem, arr. H
 of old melody
W: Nahum Tate

While swiftly the tide
WHITE PLUME, THE: see In war's stern
 panoply
Who is like unto Thee?
Who trusts in God, a strong abode

W: R. Reece   Duet

W: Exodus 15   PS
T: Constance   H
W: tr. by Benjamin
 H. Kennedy

Why shouldn't we
WILL HE COME?: see "I can scarcely
 hear," she murmur'd
WILLOW SONG, THE: see FIVE SHAKE-
 SPEARE SONGS
Wind is now weary, The
Wind now is weary, The
WINDOW, THE, or THE SONG OF THE
 WRENS; a cycle of 12 songs by Tennyson.
  1. ON THE HILL: The lights and shadows
   fly!
  2. AT THE WINDOW: Vine, vine and
   eglantine
  3. GONE: Gone! gone, till the end of
   the year
  4. WINTER: The frost is here
  5. SPRING: Birds' love and birds' song
  6. THE LETTER: Where is another
   sweet as my sweet?
  7. NO ANSWER: The mist and the rain
  8. NO ANSWER: Winds are loud
  9. THE ANSWER: Two little hands that
   meet
  10. AY: Be merry, all birds, to-day
  11. WHEN: Sun comes, moon comes
  12. MARRIAGE MORNING: Light, so
   low upon earth
Winds are loud: see THE WINDOW, no. 8
WINTER: see THE WINDOW, no. 4

W: Rosabel

W: Chas. J. Rowe
W: Chas. J. Rowe

Winter reigneth o'er the land

T: Clarence, arr.   H
W: Bp. W. Walsham
How

With the sweet word of peace

T: Parting, arr.   H
old melody
W: George Watson

With voice and solemn music: see
    IMPERIAL INSTITUTE ODE

Wreaths for our graves

W: L. F. Massey   PS

Yea, though I walk through the valley
    (from THE LIGHT OF THE WORLD,
    see Index I)

W: arr. by W. M.
Richardson

YOU SLEEP (E TU NOL SAI): see Moon
no longer rules on high, The

YOUNG MOTHER, THE; Three simple songs
    1. CRADLE SONG, OR LITTLE DARLING,
       SLEEP AGAIN: The days are cold, the
       nights are long
    2. AY DE MI, MY BIRD: O bird that
       used to press

W: George Eliot

    3. THE FIRST DEPARTURE: How
       grand, oh sea (same tune with
       different words: THE CHORISTER:

W: E. Monro

       O sweet and dim the light and shade
       W: F. E. Weatherly)

DETROIT STUDIES IN MUSIC BIBLIOGRAPHY

. . . . Bruno Nettl, General Editor

A series devoted to the publication of bibliographical contributions - mono-
graphs, essays, and special indexes, lists, and directories - prepared on all
aspects of music and its performance by recognized scholars. Its scope is
broad and limited only by bibliographical interests.

The frequency of publication, now projected at six numbers yearly, will be
determined by the availability of material, the length of manuscripts ac-
cepted, and the reception given to the series by librarians, musicians,
musicologists, and students.

Number 1 REFERENCE MATERIALS IN ETHNOMUSICOLOGY
          by Bruno Nettl, Wayne State University
          1961   46p $1.50
          A bibliographic essay which organizes,
          describes, and evaluates the basic books
          and articles on primitive, oriental, and
          folk music